PHILIP JODIDIO

NL
ARCHITECTURE IN THE NETHERLANDS

TASCHEN

KÖLN LONDON LOS ANGELES MADRID PARIS TOKYO

#1

#12

#4
5/14

#4/8/12/14
#6
#13

#3

#2

#11

#8
#5

#1/9

#11

#6/7

#10

#2

#3

#13

#1

INTRODUCTION

FROM REMBRANDT TO REM

Dutch architecture and design are hot. Beneath an outward appearance of dullness or dryness lies an adventurous heart, and a willingness to go where few creators have gone before them. Rotterdam's own Rem Koolhaas (OMA) straddles the globe much like his huge new CCTV Tower will soon straddle Beijing, while his younger colleagues, such as Lars Spuybroek (NOX) imagine houses that sing and dance. Nor does Dutch inventiveness stop at pure architecture. Droog Design does furniture, and West 8 creates gardens all over the world. Though predictions are made regularly about the end of this "golden age" of Dutch architecture, each year brings a remarkable new crop of projects and completed buildings, confirming this small nation as one of the real creative leaders in Europe, if not the world. As Aaron Betsky, the director of the Netherlands Architecture Institute in Rotterdam wrote in his recent book *False Flat, Why Dutch Design is so Good*, "Dutch architects such as MVRDV are exporting the lessons they learned designing social housing all over the world, and Dutch industrial, graphic and furniture designers are picking up commissions in the United States, Europe and Asia. In the recent competition for redesigning Ground Zero in New York, three of the seven teams included Dutch architects ... For a small country, the Netherlands exerts amazing influence." Nor is this positive attitude toward the Netherlands reserved to the already famous. Burton Hamfelt, a Canadian who is one of the principals of S 333, a young Amsterdam firm made up almost entirely of foreigners, says, "The Netherlands was a strategic choice to open an office for us; location, work climate, an enthusiastic design culture—our mixed backgrounds made this the most interesting location to also explore the world. The Netherlands is promoted as a kind of Hollywood for architects. If you want to become an actor, you go to Hollywood; if you want to become an architect, you come here. Even though the situation is clearly different now, there is still no other country where the design culture is omnipresent." Whether the best is yet to come is a moot point, in any case, Dutch architecture is here, now.

MASTERS OF THE SEA

The Dutch have a long history of commerce and power. Under Prince Maurice of Orange (1567–1625), the Republic of the United Netherlands became the greatest sea power in the world. The country was a center of trade in the 17th century. Situated on the sea and crossed by the Rhine and the Maas, two of Europe's most important waterways, from which a network of canals spread across the country, traffic and communication were easier than in any other European nation. A simplicity and a Puritan spirit born in part of the Calvinist revolution gave confidence to a bold and adventurous navy, just as it may have contributed to the rise of the remarkable artists of the period. Rembrandt, Vermeer, Hals, Saenredam, Van Ruysdael and so many others were the standard-bearers of the country's golden age. Yet, conditions of economic prosperity do not always engender artistic excellence, and scholars still debate about the reasons for which such a high concentration of great artists emerged in the Netherlands of the 17th century. The same is true of today's architectural and design talent. Reasons can be underlined, but the full explanation for the emergence of the Dutch as a powerhouse of world architecture lies somewhere beneath or behind the facts.

The history of the Netherlands has a great deal to do with the country's never-ending struggle against the sea. Roughly 2000 years ago, a Teutonic tribe known as the Frisians (or Friesians) settled in what is now the Netherlands and began to build *terpen*, and later dykes to hold back the water. In 1287, the dykes that held back the North Sea failed, and a new bay, called the Zuiderzee was created where there had been farmland. Over the centuries, the Dutch worked to slowly push back the water of the Zuiderzee, building dykes and creating polders (the term used to describe any land reclaimed from water). The floods of 1916 incited the country to start a major project to reclaim the Zuiderzee. Between 1927 and 1932, a thirty-kilometer-long structure called the Afsluitdijk (Barrier Dyke) was built, turning the Zuiderzee into the IJsselmeer, a freshwater lake. Further dykes were built, reclaiming the land of the IJsselmeer and, on January 1, 1986, the province of Flevoland was created on what had been under water for centuries. Two of the new cities where a number of today's talented architects have been called on to participate in master plans and urban development, Almere and Lelystad, are located in Flevoland.

Today, approximately 27 percent of the Netherlands is actually below sea level. This area is home to over 60 percent of the country's population. With a population of 16 318 000 (July 2004 est.) and a land area of just 33 883 km^2 or approximately the combined size of the U.S. states Connecticut and Massachusetts, the Netherlands has a population density even higher than that of Japan. Perhaps because the Dutch are amongst the few nations in the world to have willfully and continually added to the land surface of their country, without resorting to violence, it may be that they have a more pronounced sense of their own capacity to influence urban development than people from other countries. Then, too, the density of the population has created a sense of urgency in the post-War period that larger countries like France have not felt in the same way. These facts of the very existence of the Netherlands have a real impact on the situation of its architecture, beginning with an overall scheme, promulgated by the government, in collaboration with private-sector partners, and known as Vinex.

CARING FOR THE GREEN HEART

The term Randstad Holland was coined in the 1930s to denote a group of cities located in a horseshoe-shaped area, with a diameter of about 60 kilometers, including Amsterdam, Rotterdam, The Hague and Utrecht. The rural zone between these cities was named the Green Heart since the development of the country had concentrated farming and, more recently, leisure pursuits there. As early as 1958, a government report called "The West of the Country" raised the issue of urban congestion in Randstad Holland. In 1960, the first "Policy Document on Town and Country Planning" encouraged the development of peripheral areas in the northern, southern and eastern Netherlands, and the active preservation of the Green Heart, mainly because of its importance as an agricultural zone. A second policy document was published in 1966 and encouraged growth in areas such as North Holland and Flevoland. This government initiative was given a sense of urgency by the increasing encroachment of urbanization on the Green Heart, and predictions that the country's population would exceed twenty million persons by the turn of the century. Despite this early and continued interest in the development of the country, existing trends, including decreasing population in the major cities and urbanization of formerly rural areas, prevailed until more forceful action was taken. The "Policy Document on Urbanization" published in 1976 designated fourteen growth centers for the country, eleven of which were located outside of the Randstad. Despite some success, the idea of growth centers was abandoned with the "Fourth Policy Document on Town and Country Planning" published in 1988, and revised in 1990. The so-called Vinex plan called for the creation of no less than 750 000 housing units or apartments between 1995 and 2015 in twenty designated locations, including the areas around new cities in Flevoland.

Though the Vinex schemes have been criticized in many quarters, they have given rise to some particularly successful programs modeled to some extent on the housing developments seen in earlier years in the United States. For all their repetitive dullness, the housing projects generated all over the Netherlands and often supported by the government have been an occasion for young talents to emerge and to express themselves, while other countries limit their new architecture to tiny commercial venues, for example. Where talented architects like MVRDV have been called on (in Ypenburg for example), a higher standard of architectural design than that seen almost anywhere else in the world in similar circumstances has been achieved. Then again, despite clinging to laughably kitsch forms of architecture in many instances, the Netherlands appears to be more fully receptive to modernity than most of its European neighbors, perhaps because of its long tradition of openness to the outside world. This is, after all, also the country of Piet Mondrian, one of the inventors of abstraction. Today, an important source of the continuing permeability of the Netherlands is Rotterdam. Although it was founded in 1328, Rotterdam was little more than a herring fishing village in the early 17th century, when Rembrandt was born in Leiden. Trade brought it prosperity, but it was not until after 1872, when the Nieuwe Waterweg was built to keep the city and port of Rotterdam accessible to seafaring vessels (the natural Maas-Rhine branches had silted up), that it became a truly significant center. All but destroyed during World War II, Rotterdam emerged to become the largest port in the world, surpassed only today by Shanghai. It may not be entirely a coincidence that the city is now, more than Amsterdam or The Hague, the center of contemporary architecture in the Netherlands. With the flow of trade and obligatory openness to the outside world, complemented by a very high percentage of English-speakers, the city has embraced the modernity forced on it, too, by the devastation of the war.

DELIRIOUS ROTTERDAM

Rotterdam is the city not only of the most famous of contemporary Dutch architects, Rem Koolhaas (OMA), but also younger practices, such as that of Erick van Egeraat, MVRDV, Neutelings Riedijk, NOX, or Kas Oosterhuis (ONL). Koolhaas has of course had an enormous influence on the emergence of an entire generation of Dutch and foreign architects who have worked at one time or another in his office. This is the case of Kees Christaanse, Winy Maas and Jacob van Rijs (MVRDV), Willem Jan Neutelings (Neutelings Riedijk) and Mike Guyer (Gigon & Guyer). In his interesting study *SuperDutch* (London, 2000), Bart Lootsma points out that cultural institutions in the Netherlands have played a significant role in the opening-up of the Dutch architectural scene. He cites the Rotterdam Arts Council, responsible for the organization of the Architecture International of Rotterdam (AIR) that sought as early as 1982 to ask foreign architects for advice on the Kop van Zuid redevelopment zone just across the water from the city center, as an important factor. Today, the Kop van Zuid is approaching the end of its redevelopment, and such architects as Bolles & Wilson, De Architecten Cie., West 8, Van Berkel & Bos (now UN Studio), or Lord Norman Foster have worked there.

Koolhaas of course began his rise before he had built anything. His bestselling 1978 book *Delirious New York* laid down the premises of his thinking about urbanism in a congested, capitalist environment. Winner of the 2000 Pritzker Prize, and the 2003 Praemium Imperiale, Koolhaas and his office OMA have built small works like the Villa dall'Ava (Saint-Cloud, 1985-91) and have overseen large projects like the Euralille complex in Lille (1988). Today, they have signed Prada boutiques in New York and Los Angeles, built the Seattle Public Library (2004), and are advancing quickly on the 575 000m2 Headquarters and Cultural Center for China Central Television (CCTV) in Beijing. In the Netherlands, OMA is in charge of the master plan for the city center of Almere and has recently completed the Souterrain in The Hague published in this volume. Aside from forming numerous influential architects, OMA has challenged ways of thinking about architecture and urbanism on a global scale, perhaps profiting from the experience of the dense and rich Dutch environment to go on from there. Bart Lootsma points out the particular attachment of Koolhaas to one aspect of OMA's work—its "inexpensiveness." He quotes Koolhaas, who says, "There are indeed two sorts of minimalism: a Calcutta minimalism and a detailed, even fussy minimalism. I feel more affinity with Calcutta... It absolutely doesn't mean that we only make cheap things, but I think that the research into how you can carry out as many programs as possible with as little money as possible is incredibly interesting." This comment of course reminds some that the Dutch have a reputation for being "cheap." One confirmed architect in Rotterdam explains in all seriousness that much of the success of young designers in the Netherlands has to do with precisely this tendency. "Obviously," he says, if you are a promoter, "you look favorably on a younger, less expensive designer than a famous expensive one." Rather than cheapness, which can be construed as an insult, it would be more appropriate to speak of the economy of means regularly demonstrated by Dutch architects. Whether obliged by promoters or not, droog design (dry design) is deeply rooted in the Calvinist traditions of the Netherlands.

WHY THE NETHERLANDS?

Fourteen architects have been selected for this volume, but the intention is neither to sum up the creativity of the Netherlands, nor to be exhaustive in any sense of the term. These are architects who have contributed to the current reputation of Dutch architecture. Some of them (like OMA) hardly need to be introduced to readers familiar with contemporary architecture. Others (like SeARCH) are not well known outside of professional circles. The intention is to give an impression, an overview of what is currently happening in architecture in the Netherlands. All of the projects in this book are located within the country, no matter how spectacular the work of some outside of the Netherlands may be. This selection does show the continuing emphasis of the country on housing and the development of newer areas, such as the city center of Almere (master plan by OMA) or Lelystad (master plan by West 8). Some of this work shows an austerity or a dryness that may be disconcerting to those who have not looked closely at the variety and inventiveness that characterizes the buildings. On the other hand, other architects like Lars Spuybroek (NOX) and Kas Oosterhuis (ONL) have chosen to delve fully

into the realm of computer design. Their shapes and methods challenge the assumptions that underlie the very foundations of architecture. With parametric modeling and computer-driven machining of parts, an infinite variety of forms are being added by them and by like-minded architects in other countries to the repertory of building design. Many of the buildings seen in this book were designed and built with limited budgets. The Hague is not quite Calcutta, but an attention to cost is one factor that is common to almost all Dutch architecture.

Long ago, in the 17th century, the painters of Holland looked closely at themselves and painted the reality of their own existence with a simplicity and a beauty that still touches people all over the world. The face of Rembrandt and the light of Vermeer are a part of our culture. This frankness, this openness still inform the creativity of the Netherlands, despite all of its modern problems, ranging from population density to more recent questions related to race and religion. The point is not to compare Rembrandt to Rem, but for a certain time, conditions in the Netherlands have again permitted a flowering of creativity, which touches architecture and design in the larger sense. It can only be hoped that this example will continue in the future to inspire younger creators.

Philip Jodidio

EINLEITUNG

VON REMBRANDT BIS REM

Niederländische Architektur und Design sind aufregend. Unter ihrer glanzlosen, manchmal etwas rauen Schale stecken abenteuerliche Ideen und verbirgt sich der Wille von niederländischen Entwerfern zu neuen Wegen, die kaum jemand zuvor beschritten hat. Der Rotterdamer Rem Koolhaas (OMA) setzt architektonische Meilensteine in aller Welt, z. B. demnächst mit seinem gewaltigen CCTV Tower in Peking, während seine jüngeren Kollegen – wie etwa Lars Spuybroek (NOX) – sich Häuser ausdenken, die singen und tanzen. Die Erfindungskraft der Niederländer beschränkt sich aber nicht nur auf die Architektur. Droog Design entwerfen Möbel, und West 8 gestalten Gärten rund um den Globus. Trotz regelmäßiger Vorhersagen über das baldige Ende dieses „goldenen Zeitalters" der niederländischen Architektur gibt es jedes Jahr eine neue Ernte von Entwürfen und fertig gestellten Bauten als Bestätigung der Tatsache, dass dieses kleine Land in kreativer Hinsicht in Europa – wenn nicht gar weltweit – führend ist. In seinem vor Kurzem veröffentlichten Buch *False Flat. Why Dutch Design is so Good*, schreibt Aaron Betsky, Direktor des Niederländischen Architekturinstituts in Rotterdam: „Niederländische Architekturbüros wie MVRDV exportieren in alle Welt, was sie beim Bau von Sozialwohnungen gelernt haben, und niederländische Industrie-, Grafik- und Möbeldesigner erhalten Aufträge in den Vereinigten Staaten, Europa und Asien. Beim Wettbewerb für die Neubebauung des Ground Zero in New York waren Niederländer in drei der sieben teilnehmenden Architektenteams beteiligt ... Das Land ist zwar klein, aber erstaunlich einflussreich." Diese positive Einschätzung der Niederlande betrifft nicht nur ihre Berühmtheiten. Der Kanadier Burton Hamfelt, einer der leitenden Partner des jungen Amsterdamer Architekturbüros S 333, in dem fast nur Ausländer arbeiten, sagt beispielsweise: „Die Niederlande waren für uns aufgrund von Standort, Arbeitsklima und äußerst lebendiger Designkultur das Land der Wahl für eine Niederlassung. Da wir aus verschiedenen Ländern stammen, können wir von hier aus die Welt am besten erkunden. Die Niederlande sind eine Art Hollywood für Architekten. Als Schauspieler geht man nach Hollywood, als Architekt kommt man hierher. Die Situation hat sich zwar verändert, aber es gibt immer noch kein anderes Land, in dem die Designkultur so allgegenwärtig ist." Ob das Beste noch vor uns liegt, ist strittig, auf jeden Fall ist die niederländische Architektur hier und heute präsent.

DIE BEHERRSCHER DER MEERE

Die Niederländer blicken auf eine lange Handels- und Herrschaftsgeschichte zurück. Unter ihrem Statthalter Prinz Moritz von Oranien (1567 – 1625) entwickelte sich die Republik der Vereinigten Niederlande zur größten Seemacht der Welt. Im 17. Jahrhundert war das Land ein führender Handelsplatz. Es lag nicht nur am Meer, sondern wurde auch noch von Rhein und Maas, den zwei wichtigsten Wasserwegen Europas, durchzogen, von denen aus sich ein Netz von Kanälen über das Land ausbreitete, so dass Verkehr und Kommunikation hier leichter vonstatten gingen als anderswo. Die Vorliebe für Einfachheit und der puritanische Geist – zum Teil Folgen des Kalvinismus – trugen zum Selbstbewusstsein einer kühnen, abenteuerlustigen Marine und vielleicht auch zum Erfolg der großen Künstler jener Zeit bei. Rembrandt, Vermeer, Hals, Saenredam, Van Ruysdael und viele andere waren die Standartenträger des goldenen Zeitalters der Niederlande. Wirtschaftlicher Wohlstand fördert jedoch nicht immer auch hervorragende künstlerische Qualität, und die Historiker streiten sich immer noch über die Gründe für die „Häufung" herausragender Künstler in den Niederlanden des 17. Jahrhunderts. Gleiches gilt für die Architekten und Designer der Gegenwart. Auch für die Entwicklung des Landes zu einer Quelle der Inspiration für die Weltarchitektur schlummern die tatsächlichen Gründe irgendwo hinter oder unter den Fakten.

Vieles in der Geschichte der Niederlande hat damit zu tun, dass die Bewohner ihr Land ständig gegen das Meer verteidigen mussten. Vor rund 2000 Jahren besiedelte der Germanenstamm der Friesen die heutigen Niederlande und baute Deiche zum Schutz vor den Fluten der Nordsee. 1287 brachen die Deiche und eine neue Bucht – die Zuidersee – entstand, wo vorher Ackerland gewesen war. Über Jahrhunderte arbeiteten die Niederländer beharrlich daran, das Meer wieder zurückzudrängen, indem sie Deiche bauten und Polder aufschütteten, und so trotzten sie dem Meer neues Land ab. Nach der Flutkatastrophe von 1916 lancierte die Regierung das Vorhaben, das von der Zuidersee überflutete Land teilweise wiederzugewinnen. Von 1927 bis 1932 wurde der 30 km lange Afsluitdijk (Abschlussdeich) gebaut. Dieser machte die Zuidersee zum riesigen Süßwassersee, dem IJsselmeer. Weitere Deiche wurden gebaut und Polder angelegt, so dass am 1. Januar 1986 die neue Provinz Flevoland entstand, wo Jahrhunderte lang nur Wasser gewesen war. Almere und Lelystad gehören zu den neuen Städten der Provinz, an deren Planung und Bau viele der talentierten zeitgenössischen Architekten beteiligt waren.

Heute liegen rund 27 % des Landes unterhalb des Meeresspiegels. In diesem Gebiet leben aber über 60 % der Niederländer. Bei einer Bevölkerungszahl von rund 16,3 Millionen (Juli 2004) und einem Staatsgebiet von nur 33 883 km², was ungefähr der Größe der US-Staaten Connecticut und Massachusetts zusammen entspricht, haben die Niederlande eine noch höhere Bevölkerungsdichte als Japan. Vielleicht verdanken die Niederländer ihren ausgeprägten Glauben an die Machbarkeit urbaner Entwicklungen der Tatsache, dass sie zu den wenigen Nationen gehören, die ihr nationales Territorium beharrlich und gezielt vergrößert haben, ohne Gewalt gegenüber anderen Völkern anzuwenden. Hinzu kommt, dass die Bevölkerungsdichte in der Nachkriegszeit Stadtplanung und Wohnungsbau zu dringenderen Problemen machte als es etwa in Frankreich der Fall war. Diese der Existenz der Niederlande zugrunde liegenden Fakten haben reale Auswirkungen auf die Architektur des Landes, allen voran der Raumordnungsplan unter dem Namen Vinex, der von der Regierung in Kooperation mit der privaten Bauwirtschaft initiiert wurde.

SORGE UM DAS „GRÜNE HERZ"

Der Begriff „Randstad Holland" kam in den 1930er Jahren als Bezeichnung für das hufeisenförmige, rund 60 km durchmessende Ballungsgebiet der Westniederlande auf, in dem Amsterdam, Rotterdam, Den Haag und Utrecht liegen. Im Zentrum der Randstad befindet sich das „grüne Herz" mit den größten zusammenhängenden landwirtschaftlichen Flächen und natürlichen Erholungsgebieten des Landes. Schon 1958 beschäftigte sich ein Regierungsbericht zum „Westen des Landes" mit dem Problem der Verstädterung der Randstad Holland. 1960 wurden die ersten Richtlinien zur Stadt- und Regionalplanung verabschiedet, welche die Entwicklung städtischer Randgebiete im Norden, Süden und Osten der Niederlande und den Erhalt der grünen Mitte (vor allem als wichtiges landwirtschaftliches Gebiet) vorschrieben. 1966 folgte eine zweite Richtlinie zur Förderung städtischen Wachstums, u. a. in Nordholland und Flevoland. Diese Regierungsinitiative war dringend notwendig, weil der Siedlungsdruck auf die grüne Mitte stark zugenommen hatte und weil für die Jahrhundertwende eine Bevölkerungszahl von über 20 Millionen prognostiziert worden war. Trotz dieser frühzeitigen und anhaltenden Sorge um die Landes- und Stadtentwicklung setzten sich bereits bestehende Trends wie etwa sinkende Einwohnerzahlen in den Großstädten und die Zersiedlung der Landschaft fort, bis die Regierung wirksamere Maßnahmen ergriff. Die vierte Richtlinie zur Stadt- und Regionalplanung wurde 1988 verabschiedet und 1990 überarbeitet. Das so genannte Vinex-Programm forderte den Bau von nicht weniger als 750 000 Häusern und Wohnungen im Zeitraum von 1995 bis 2015 an 20 festgelegten Standorten, einschließlich der Randgebiete der neuen Städte in Flevoland.

Zwar sind die Vinex-Pläne vielfach kritisiert worden, sie haben aber auch eine Reihe besonders gelungener Beispiele hervorgebracht, die bis zu einem gewissen Grad dem Vorbild früherer Siedlungsprojekte in den USA folgten. Obwohl es oft triste, eintönige Siedlungen hervorbrachte, bot das landesweite, teils staatlich geförderte Wohnungsbauprogramm jungen Architekten eine Chance, sich zu profilieren und neue Ideen zu realisieren, während sie sich in anderen

Ländern vielfach auf kleine kommerzielle Bauten beschränken müssen. Wo talentierte Architekten wie MVRDV eingeschaltet wurden – etwa in Ypenburg –, erreichte man ein höheres architektonisches Niveau als unter vergleichbaren Umständen irgendwo sonst auf der Welt. Trotz vieler Fälle einer geradezu lächerlich kitschigen Architektur in den Niederlanden scheint man dort wesentlich aufgeschlossener gegenüber modernen Ausdrucksformen zu sein als in den meisten anderen Ländern Europas. Vielleicht liegt das an der langen Tradition der Weltoffenheit des Landes. Immerhin ist es das Land Piet Mondrians, der zu den Erfindern der abstrakten Kunst zählt. Heutzutage verdanken die Niederlande ihre anhaltende Aufgeschlossenheit insbesondere Rotterdam. Zwar wurde die Stadt schon 1328 gegründet, war aber nicht viel mehr als ein Heringsfischerdorf, als Rembrandt 1606 in Leiden zur Welt kam. Durch Handel gelangte Rotterdam zu Wohlstand, zum wirklich bedeutenden Handelsplatz entwickelte sich die Stadt aber erst nach dem Bau des Nieuwe Waterweg (1872), der notwendig geworden war, weil die natürlichen Flussbetten von Rhein und Maas zunehmend versandeten. Dieser Kanal machte die Stadt und den Hafen für große Passagier- und Frachtschiffe zugänglich. Im Zweiten Weltkrieg fast völlig zerstört, entwickelte sich Rotterdam in der Folge zum größten Hafen der Welt (inzwischen dem zweitgrößten nach Schanghai). Es ist sicher kein reiner Zufall, dass die Stadt heute vor Amsterdam und Den Haag das Zentrum der zeitgenössischen niederländischen Architektur ist. Der Welthandel brachte Weltoffenheit sowie einen hohen Prozentsatz Englisch sprechender Bürger mit sich, und die Stadt hat sich inzwischen die durch Kriegszerstörung erzwungene Modernität bewusst zu Eigen gemacht.

VERRÜCKTES ROTTERDAM

Rotterdam ist nicht nur die Stadt des berühmtesten zeitgenössischen Architekten der Niederlande, Rem Koolhaas, sondern auch Sitz der Büros vieler jüngerer Kollegen wie Erick van Egeraat, MVRDV, Neutelings Riedijk, NOX und Kas Oosterhuis (ONL). Natürlich hat Koolhaas eine ganze Generation von Architekten aus dem In- und Ausland geprägt, die über die Jahre in einem seiner Büros gearbeitet haben, u. a. Kees Christiaanse, Winy Maas und Jacob van Rijs (MVRDV), Willem Jan Neutelings (Neutelings Riedijk) und Mike Guyer (Gigon & Guyer). In seiner interessanten Studie *SuperDutch* (London, 2000) weist Bart Lootsma darauf hin, dass kulturelle Institutionen bei der Entwicklung der niederländischen Architektur eine wichtige Rolle gespielt haben, und führt als ein Beispiel den Rotterdamer Kunstrat an, Veranstalter der Architektur-Internationale Rotterdam (AIR), die schon 1982 ausländische Architekten als Berater zur Entwicklung des Gebiets Kop van Zuid (vom Stadtzentrum gesehen jenseits des Wassers) heranzog. Heute steht das neue Stadtviertel kurz vor der Fertigstellung, und Architekten wie Bolles & Wilson,

De Architecten Cie., Van Berkel & Bos (heute UN Studio) oder Lord Norman Foster haben dort gebaut.

Koolhaas wurde berühmt, bevor er irgend etwas gebaut hatte. In seinem 1978 erschienenen Bestseller *Delirious New York* legte er seine Auffassung vom Städtebau in einem übervölkerten kapitalistischen Umfeld dar. Koolhaas und sein Büro OMA – Pritzker-Preisträger des Jahres 2000 und Gewinner des Praemium Imperiale 2003 – haben so kleine Bauten realisiert wie die Villa dall'Ava (Saint-Cloud, 1985–91) und so große Projekte betreut wie das Euralille-Viertel in Lille (1988). OMA hat Prada-Boutiquen in New York und Los Angeles gestaltet, die Seattle Public Library errichtet (2004) und baut derzeit das 575 000 m² umfassende Verwaltungs- und Kulturzentrum des chinesischen Fernsehsenders CCTV in Peking. In den Niederlanden hat Koolhaas den Masterplan für das neue Stadtzentrum von Almere entworfen und vor Kurzem den in diesem Buch beschriebenen „Souterrain"-Verkehrsbau in Den Haag fertig gestellt. OMA hat nicht nur zahlreiche, heute einflussreiche Architekten geprägt, sondern international auch herkömmliche Auffassungen von Architektur und Städtebau infrage gestellt und dabei aus der eigenen Erfahrung mit der vielfältigen gebauten Umwelt der Niederlande geschöpft. Bart Lootsma spricht von Koolhaas' besonderer Vorliebe für einen spezifischen Aspekt seiner OMA-Bauten – ihre „Billigkeit" – und zitiert Koolhaas selbst: „Es gibt tatsächlich zwei Arten von Minimalismus, den vom Typ Kalkutta und einen detailreichen, geradezu pingeligen Minimalismus. Mir liegt der Kalkutta-Minimalismus näher! Das heißt keineswegs, dass wir nur billig bauen, aber ich finde es unglaublich interessant zu erforschen, wie man mit möglichst wenig Geld möglichst viele Programme bauen kann." Diese Bemerkung erinnert uns daran, dass die Niederländer im Ruf stehen, „billig" zu arbeiten. Ein anerkannter Rotterdamer Architekt hat allen Ernstes erklärt, der Erfolg seiner jungen Kollegen und Landsleute sei zum großen Teil genau darauf zurückzuführen. Natürlich, sagt er, würden Investoren sich eher einen jüngeren Architekten suchen, der für weniger Honorar arbeitet, als einen berühmten, der viel verlangt. Statt von „Billigkeit" zu reden – was man auch als Beleidigung auslegen kann – sollte man besser über die von niederländischen Architekten vielfach geübte Sparsamkeit der Mittel sprechen. Ob von Bauinvestoren dazu verpflichtet oder nicht, Droog Design (wörtlich: trockenes Design) ist tief in der kalvinistischen Tradition der Niederlande verwurzelt.

WARUM DIE NIEDERLANDE?

In diesem Band werden 14 Architekten vorgestellt, ohne dass damit die gesamte architektonische Kreativität der Niederlande zusammengefasst oder nur annähernd erschöpfend behandelt werden kann. Die ausgewählten Büros haben alle zum gegenwärtigen guten Ruf der zeitgenössischen Architektur des Landes beigetragen. Einige (wie etwa OMA) müssen Lesern, die sich in der Architektur auskennen, nicht extra vorgestellt werden; andere (wie z. B. SeARCH) sind außerhalb des Berufsstands noch relativ unbekannt. Dieses Buch soll einen Eindruck vom gegenwärtigen Baugeschehen in den Niederlanden vermitteln und lässt daher die im Ausland realisierten Projekte niederländischer Architekten außer Acht, so atemberaubend sie auch sein mögen. Die Auswahl verdeutlicht aber, dass das Land sich nach wie vor auf den Wohnungsbau und Stadtentwicklungsprojekte, einschließlich den Bau neuer Stadtzentren wie Almere (Masterplan von OMA) oder Lelystad (Masterplan von West 8) konzentriert. Einige dieser Bauten sind von einer Strenge oder Nüchternheit, die all jene abschrecken mag, die sie nur flüchtig betrachten und dabei die Originalität und den Variationsreichtum des Entwurfs übersehen. Andere Architekten wie Lars Spuybroek (NOX) und Kas Oosterhuis (ONL) haben sich konsequent dem Entwerfen am Computer verschrieben. Ihre Formen und Techniken stellen genau die Postulate infrage, welche die Grundfesten der Architektur bilden. Mit parametrischer Formgebung und computergestützter Fertigung von Bauteilen erweitern sie und gleichgesinnte Architekten in anderen Ländern das architektonische Repertoire um eine Vielzahl neuer Formen. Eine ganze Reihe der in diesem Buch vorgestellten Gebäude sind mit begrenzten Mitteln realisiert worden. Den Haag ist zwar nicht ganz so wie Kalkutta, aber Kostenbewusstsein bzw. Kostenreduzierung spielt bei fast allen Neubauten in den Niederlanden eine große Rolle.

Die niederländischen Maler des 17. Jahrhunderts waren aufmerksame Beobachter und malten sich selbst und ihre Lebenswelt mit einer Klarheit und Schönheit, die Menschen in aller Welt noch heute ansprechen. Rembrandts Gesicht und Vermeers Licht sind Teil unserer Kultur. Diese Klarheit und Offenheit prägen auch heute noch das künstlerische und architektonische Schaffen in den Niederlanden, trotz aller modernen Probleme des Landes – von der Bevölkerungsdichte bis zu den aktuellen ethnischen und religiösen Konflikten. Man kann Rembrandt nicht mit Rem vergleichen, Tatsache aber ist, dass die Niederlande seit etlichen Jahren erneut eine kreative Blütezeit erleben, die sich in Architektur und Design im weitesten Sinne manifestiert. Es ist zu hoffen, dass dieses Beispiel auch in Zukunft jüngere Talente inspirieren wird.

Philip Jodidio

INTRODUCTION

DE REMBRANDT À REM

L'architecture et le design néerlandais sont en pleine effervescence. Sous une apparence un peu sèche voire ennuyeuse bat un cœur audacieux et un goût pour s'aventurer vers des régions que peu de créateurs ont explorées jusqu'alors. Rem Koolhaas (OMA), l'enfant prodige de Rotterdam, a planté son fanion sur le globe un peu comme son énorme tour CCTV va bientôt le faire sur Pékin, tandis que ses confrères plus jeunes, comme Lars Spuybroek (NOX), imaginent des maisons qui chantent et qui dansent. L'inventivité néerlandaise ne s'arrête pas à l'architecture pure. Droog Design fait des meubles et West 8 crée des jardins pour le monde entier. Bien que l'on prédise régulièrement la fin de ce nouvel « âge d'or » de l'architecture néerlandaise, chaque année apporte une remarquable moisson de projets et de réalisations qui confirment la place d'un des grands leaders de la création européenne, sinon mondiale, qu'occupe de cette petite nation. Comme Aaron Betsky, directeur de l'Institut néerlandais de l'architecture de Rotterdam l'écrivait dans son récent ouvrage *False Flat, Why Dutch Design is so Good* (Faux-plat, pourquoi la conception néerlandaise est si bonne) : « Les architectes néerlandais comme MVRDV exportent les leçons qu'ils ont apprises en concevant des logements sociaux pour le monde entier, et les designers industriels, les créateurs de mobilier ou les graphistes ramassent les commandes aussi bien aux États-Unis et en Europe qu'en Asie. Dans le récent concours pour Ground Zero à New York, trois des sept équipes en compétition comprenaient des architectes néerlandais ... Pour un petit pays, les Pays-Bas exercent une étonnante influence. » Cette attitude positive envers les Pays-Bas n'est pas réservée qu'aux célébrités. Le Canadien Burton Hamfelt qui est l'un des dirigeants de S 333 une jeune agence d'Amsterdam presque entièrement composée d'étrangers déclare : « Ouvrir un bureau aux Pays-Bas était pour nous un choix stratégique. Lieu, travail, climat, culture du design enthousiaste et nos origines mélangées, tout en faisait une localisation idéale pour explorer le monde. Les Pays-Bas sont présentés comme une sorte d'Hollywood pour architectes. Si vous voulez devenir acteur, vous allez à Hollywood, mais si vous voulez devenir architecte, vous venez ici. Même si, clairement, la situation est différente aujourd'hui, il n'existe aucun autre pays dans lequel la culture du design soit aussi omniprésente. » Que le meilleur soit encore à venir est sujet à controverse, mais l'architecture néerlandaise est bien là, ici et maintenant.

MAÎTRES DES MERS

Les Néerlandais possèdent une longue histoire de puissance commerciale mondiale. Au XVIIᵉ siècle, sous le prince Maurice d'Orange (1567 – 1625), la république des Provinces-Unies devint la plus grande puissance maritime du monde et l'un des centres du commerce international. Située au bord de la mer et traversée par le Rhin et la Meuse – deux des plus importantes voies fluviales européennes d'où la présence de canaux qui sillonnaient déjà le pays – elle bénéficiait de réseaux de communication plus faciles que n'importe quelle autre nation d'Europe. La simplicité et l'esprit puritain issus en partie de la tradition calviniste donnaient la force morale nécessaire à une marine aventureuse et audacieuse, de même qu'elle a pu contribuer à l'apparition de remarquables artistes tout au long de cette période. Rembrandt, Vermeer, Hals, Saenredam, van Ruysdael et tant d'autres furent les porte-drapeaux de ce premier âge d'or. Cependant, les conditions de la prospérité économique n'engendrent pas toujours l'excellence artistique et les chercheurs se demandent encore comment une telle concentration de grands artistes a pu s'imposer dans les Pays-Bas de cette époque. Il en est de même aujourd'hui pour le talent des architectes et des designers. Certaines raisons peuvent être soulignées, mais l'explication de cette émergence des Néerlandais parmi les grandes puissances de l'architecture mondiale se cache peut-être derrière les faits.

L'histoire des Pays-Bas est très liée à l'incessant combat contre la mer. Il y a environ 2000 ans, une tribu teutonne, les Frisons, s'installa dans ce qui est aujourd'hui les Pays-Bas et commença à construire des terpen, ou digues, pour contenir les flots. En 1287, celles qui retenaient la mer du Nord se rompirent et une nouvelle baie, appelée le Zuiderzee, s'ouvrit en recouvrant des terres cultivées. Au cours des siècles, les Hollandais œuvrèrent pour repousser lentement l'eau du Zuiderzee en élevant des digues et en établissant des polders (terrains récupérés sur les eaux). Les inondations de 1916 incitèrent le pays à lancer un projet majeur de récupération du Zuiderzee. De 1927 à 1932, une structure de 32 km de long, la Afsluitdijk (la digue-barrière), fut élevée qui transforma le Zuiderzee en Ijsselmeer, un lac d'eau douce. D'autres digues furent montées pour récupérer les terrains de ce nouvel espace et le 1ᵉʳ janvier 1986, fut créée la province de Flevoland, sur des terres submergées pendant des siècles. Deux villes nouvelles de cette province, Almere et Lelystad, ont fait appel à des architectes contemporains de talent pour participer à l'élaboration d'un plan directeur et de développement urbain.

Aujourd'hui, environ 27 % des Pays-Bas sont en dessous du niveau de la mer et abritent 60 % de la population du pays qui s'élève à 16 318 000 habitants (estimation juillet 2004) sur une surface de tout juste 33 883 km², environ celle du Connecticut et du Massachusetts réunis. La densité de la population est même plus élevée que celle du Japon. C'est peut-être parce que les Néerlandais sont parmi les rares peuples au monde à avoir volontairement et continuellement accru la surface de leur pays sans recourir à la violence qu'ils possèdent un sens plus prononcé de la capacité à influencer le développement urbain. La densité démographique elle aussi a pu créer un sentiment d'urgence au cours de la période de l'après-guerre, ce que d'autres pays plus vastes, comme la France, n'ont pas ressenti de la même façon. Ces faits qui pèsent sur l'existence même de ce pays exercent un impact réel sur la situation de son architecture, comme le montre un ambitieux programme d'ensemble appelé Vinex, établi par le gouvernement en collaboration avec des partenaires du secteur privé.

LE GRAND CŒUR

Le terme de Randstad Holland fut créé dans les années 1930 pour désigner un groupe de villes situées dans une zone en fer à cheval de 60 km de diamètre environ, comprenant Amsterdam, Rotterdam, La Haye et Utrecht. La partie rurale subsistant entre ces cités fut nommée le Cœur vert, car le développement local s'était jusque là concentré sur l'agriculture et plus récemment les loisirs. Dès 1958, un rapport gouvernemental intitulé « L'Ouest du pays » avait soulevé le problème de la congestion urbaine en Randstad Holland. En 1960, le premier « Document de planification urbaine et rurale » encourageait le développement de zones périphériques au nord, au sud et à l'est du pays et la préservation active du Cœur vert, essentiellement d'ailleurs pour son importance agricole. Un second document fut publié en 1966 pour encourager la croissance dans des zones comme la Hollande du Nord et le Flevoland. En insistant sur la pression de l'urbanisation dans le Cœur vert et avec les études annonçant une population de plus de vingt millions d'habitants au tournant du siècle, cette initiative gouvernementale créa un sentiment d'urgence. Malgré cet intérêt précoce et constant pour le développement, les tendances existantes, dont la diminution de population des grandes villes et l'urbanisation d'anciennes zones rurales, prévalurent jusqu'à ce que des mesures plus directives soient prises. Le « Document de politique d'urbanisation » publié en 1976 désignait alors quatorze « centres de croissance » pour le pays dont onze étaient situés hors de Randstad. Malgré une certaine réussite, cette idée fut abandonnée par le « Quatrième document de planification urbaine et rurale », publié en 1988 et révisé en 1990. Ce plan, le Vinex, appelait à la création de pas moins de 750 000 logements entre 1995 et 2015 dans vingt lieux désignés, dont les zones autour des nouvelles villes du Flevoland.

Bien que les projets du Vinex aient été critiqués dans de nombreuses franges de l'opinion, ils ont donné naissance à quelques programmes très réussis modelés dans une certaine mesure sur des opérations de logement observées quelques années plus tôt aux États-Unis. Malgré leur répétitivité ennuyeuse, les programmes de logements réalisés dans tout le pays et souvent financés par l'État

ont été l'occasion pour de jeunes talents de se faire connaître et de s'exprimer, alors que dans d'autres pays ils en étaient souvent réduits à de petites réalisations commerciales. Lorsque des architectes reconnus comme MVRDV ont été appelés (à Ypenburg, par exemple), ces projets ont pu atteindre à un niveau de qualité architecturale plus élevé que n'importe où dans le monde ou presque, dans des circonstances similaires. Les Pays-Bas, bien que souvent amateurs de formes kitsch en architecture, semblent beaucoup plus ouverts à la modernité que la plupart de leurs voisins européens, peut-être du fait de leur longue tradition d'ouverture sur le monde extérieur. C'est après tout le pays de Piet Mondrian, l'un des inventeurs de l'abstraction. Aujourd'hui, un des centres importants de la perméabilité de ce pays aux idées est Rotterdam. Fondée en 1328, la ville n'était guère qu'un petit port de pêcheurs au début du XVIIe siècle au moment où Rembrandt naissait à Leyde. Le commerce lui apporta la prospérité mais elle dut attendre 1872, lorsque le Nieuwe Waterweg fut creusé pour maintenir l'accès de la cité et du port aux navires de mer (les bras du Rhin et la Meuse s'ensablaient), pour devenir un centre économique important. Pratiquement rasée pendant la Seconde Guerre mondiale, elle devint par la suite le second port du monde, le premier étant aujourd'hui Shanghai. Ce n'est sans doute pas un hasard si la cité est devenue, plus qu'Amsterdam ou La Haye, le centre de l'architecture contemporaine aux Pays-Bas. Avec le flux des échanges commerciaux, son ouverture sur le monde et la présence d'une population parlant anglais, la ville s'est emparée de la modernité, poussée il faut le dire par les dévastations de la guerre.

ROTTERDAM DÉLIRE

Rotterdam est non seulement le port d'attache du plus célèbre des architectes néerlandais contemporains, Rem Koolhaas (OMA), mais aussi celui d'agences plus récentes comme celle d'Erik van Egeraat, MVRDV, Neutelings Riedijk, NOX ou Kas Oosterhuis (ONL). Koolhaas a bien sûr exercé une énorme influence sur l'émergence de toute une génération d'architectes néerlandais et étrangers qui a travaillé à un moment ou un autre dans son équipe. C'est le cas de Kees Christaanse, Winy Maas et Jacob van Rijs (MVRDV), Willem Jan Neutlings (Neutlings Riedijk) ou Mike Gruyer (Gigon & Gruyer). Dans son intéressante étude intitulée *SuperDutch* (Londres, 2000), Bart Lootsma fait remarquer que les institutions culturelles des Pays-Bas ont joué un rôle significatif dans l'ouverture de la scène architecturale locale. Il cite le Conseil des Arts de Rotterdam, responsable de l'organisation de Architecture International of Rotterdam (AIR) qui, dès 1982, a demandé à des architectes étrangers leur avis sur la zone de développement de Kop van Zuid face au centre ville. Aujourd'hui le Kop van Zuid approche de la fin de sa rénovation et a bénéficié des interventions d'architectes comme Bolles &

Wilson, De Architecten Cie., West 8, Van Berkel & Bos (aujourd'hui UN Studio), ou Norman Foster.

L'ascension de Koolhaas a débuté bien avant qu'il n'ait réalisé quoi que ce soit. Son livre best-seller paru en 1978, *New York Délire*, posait les bases de sa réflexion sur l'urbanisme dans un environnement capitaliste congestionné. Titulaire du Pritzker Prize 2000 et du Praemium Imperiale 2003, Koolhaas et son agence OMA ont réalisé aussi bien de petits projets comme la Villa dall'Ava (Saint-Cloud, France 1985 – 91) que supervisé de vastes programmes comme celui du complexe Euralille à Lille (France, 1988). Récemment, il a signé des magasins Prada à New York et Los Angeles, édifié la Bibliothèque publique de Seattle (2004) tout en avançant rapidement sur les 575 000 m² du siège du Centre culturel de la Télévision Centrale Chinoise (CCTV) à Pékin. Aux Pays-Bas, OMA est en charge du plan directeur d'Almere et a récemment achevé le Souterrain, à la Haye, publié dans ces pages. Tout en formant de nombreux architectes influents, OMA a remis en question la manière de penser l'architecture et l'urbanisme à une échelle globale, profitant peut-être de l'expérience du riche et dense environnement néerlandais. Bart Lootsma note l'attachement particulier de Koolhaas à un aspect du travail d'OMA, son « esprit d'économie ». Il cite l'architecte déclarant : « ... il existe en réalité deux sortes de minimalisme, un minimalisme de Calcutta, et un minimalisme d'exécution et même mignard. Je me sens davantage d'affinités avec Calcutta ... Cela ne signifie absolument pas que nous ne faisons que des choses bon marché, mais je pense que la recherche sur les moyens de faire avancer autant de programmes que possible avec aussi peu d'argent que possible est incroyablement intéressante. » Ce commentaire en rappelle d'autres sur l'esprit d'économie des Hollandais. Un architecte confirmé de Rotterdam explique très sérieusement qu'une grande partie du succès des jeunes créateurs actuels tient à cette tendance. « À l'évidence », dit-il, « si vous êtes promoteur, vous considérez avec faveur un architecte plus jeune et moins cher qu'un autre célèbre et cher. » Plutôt que le « bon marché » qui à la limite pourrait être insultant, il serait plus approprié de parler de l'économie de moyens dont font preuve ces nouveaux architectes néerlandais. Qu'ils y soient obligés par les promoteurs ou non, le droog design (le design sec) est très enraciné dans les traditions calvinistes de ce pays.

POURQUOI LES PAYS-BAS ?

Quatorze architectes ont été sélectionnés pour cet ouvrage, mais l'intention n'est ici ni de résumer la créativité de ce pays ni d'être en aucune façon exhaustif. Il s'agit d'architectes qui ont contribué à la réputation actuelle de l'architecture néerlandaise. Certains d'entre eux, comme OMA, n'ont guère besoin d'être présentés à des lecteurs familiers de l'architecture contemporaine, mais d'autres, comme SeARCH ne sont pas encore vraiment connus hors des cercles professionnels. L'intention est donc d'offrir une impression, un survol de ce qui se passe actuellement dans ce pays précis. Tous les projets illustrés se trouvent aux Pays-Bas mêmes, quelles que soient les réalisations spectaculaires menées à l'extérieur de Randstad Holland. Ce choix montre l'accent permanent mis par ce pays sur le logement et le développement de zones nouvelles comme Almere (plan directeur de OMA) ou Lelystad (plan directeur de West 8). Certains travaux montrent une austérité et une sécheresse qui peut déconcerter mais qui disparaît à l'analyse approfondie de la variété et de l'inventivité de ces immeubles. Par ailleurs, d'autres architectes comme Lars Spuybroek (NOX) et Kas Oosterhuis (ONL) ont résolument choisi de s'engager dans le domaine de la CAO. Leurs formes et méthodes remettent en cause certains présupposés sur lesquels s'appuient les fondations mêmes de l'architecture. Grâce au paramétrage des modélisations et à la fabrication des pièces assistée par ordinateur, une variété infinie de formes est maintenant apportée par ces créateurs et leurs confrères d'autres pays au grand répertoire des formes architecturales. Un grand nombre des réalisations présentées dans les pages qui suivent ont été conçues et construites dans le cadre de budgets limités. La Haye n'est pas Calcutta, mais l'attention au coût est un facteur commun à presque toute l'architecture néerlandaise.

Il y a fort longtemps, au XVIIᵉ siècle, les peintres hollandais regardaient le milieu dans lequel ils vivaient et décrivaient la réalité de leur existence avec une simplicité et une beauté qui nous touchent encore. Le visage de Rembrandt et la lumière de Vermeer font partie de notre culture. Cette franchise, cette ouverture nourrit toujours la créativité des Pays-Bas, en dépit de tous leurs problèmes qui vont de la densité de la population à des enjeux plus récents de races et de religion. L'idée n'est pas de comparer Rembrandt et Rem, mais, pour l'instant, les conditions existantes ont à nouveau permis une explosion de créativité qui touche l'architecture et le design au sens le plus large. On ne peut qu'espérer que cet exemple continuera dans l'avenir à inspirer les futurs créateurs.

Philip Jodidio

WIEL ARETS

WIEL ARETS ARCHITECT & ASSOCIATES
D'Artagnanlaan 29
6213 CH Maastricht

Tel: +31 43 3 51 22 00
Fax: +31 43 3 21 21 92
e-mail: info@wielarets.nl
Web: www.wielarets.nl

Born in Heerlen in 1955, **WIEL ARETS** graduated from the Technical University in Eindhoven in 1983. He established Wiel Arets Architect & Associates in Heerlen the following year and moved to Maastricht in 1996. He has traveled to Russia, Japan, America and Europe (1984–89) and has taught at Academy of Architecture, Amsterdam and Rotterdam (1986–89). His interest in architectural theory led him to create the Wiederhall publishing house in 1987. Arets was a Diploma Unit Master at the Architectural Association (AA) in London (1988–92), and a Visiting Professor at Columbia University, New York (1991–92). He was Dean of the Berlage Institute, Postgraduate Laboratory of Architecture in Amsterdam (1995–98), where he was the successor of Herman Hertzberger. In 2004, he became a Professor at the University of Arts in Berlin. **BETTINA KRAUS**, born 1970 in Nuremberg, graduated from the Technical University Stuttgart in 1996, after studying at the ETH Zurich and HDK Berlin. She joined Wiel Arets Architects & Associates in 1997, and became a partner in 2000. Since 2004, she has taught at the University of Arts in Berlin. The built work of the firm includes a House & Pharmacy, Schoonbroodt, Brunssum (1985–86); Barbershop and House, Mayntz, Heerlen (1986–87); Fashionshop Beltgens, Maastricht (1987); Academy of Art and Architecture, Maastricht (1989–93); 67 apartments, Tilburg (1992–94); the Headquarters of the AZL Pensionfund, Heerlen (1990–95); a Police Station, Vaals (1993–96); 104 apartments at Jacobsplaats, Rotterdam (1995–97); and the Lensvelt Factory and Offices, Breda (1999–2000). Arets participated in the 1997 invited competition for the renovation and expansion of the Museum of Modern Art in New York. Current work includes Europol, The Hague; Transpolis Airport, Brussels; Phoenix City Project, Suzhou, China, and Servatius, Maastricht.

UNIVERSITY LIBRARY
UTRECHT 1997-2004

FLOOR AREA: 36 250 m², 4.2 million books
CLIENT: University of Utrecht
COST: €45 million

This Library is part of the new Utrecht University complex. The architect sought to resolve the inherent contradiction of the open space needed for students and researchers, and the closed space required for the storage of books and other light-sensitive collections. Arets says, "The closed volumes of the depots are suspended like opaque clouds in the air, yet the open structure gives visitors an experience of spaciousness and freedom." Vegetal patterns have become an overall theme of the design, silk-screened on the glazed façades in order to reduce the penetration of sunlight and to "create a sense of a building in the woods." The main staircase of the building leads to an auditorium and exhibition gallery, and then on to the actual library space on the first level. A void near the central desk cuts through the entire building, letting in natural light. A patio on the eastern side of the building separates the library from the five-level parking facility and assures that daylight also enters on this side. The glass façade of the car park underlines that it is part of the overall complex. As Arets describes his building, criticized by some because of its blackness, "The UBU ... is more than a place where people can consult books—it is a place where they can work in a concentrated fashion, but also one where they can meet other people without the need of any other stimuli except the atmosphere that the building radiates. The book depots, which seem to float like clouds, divide the space into zones and are interconnected by stairs and slopes. The depots in black figured concrete on which the reading rooms rest are encased by a partly double-glazed façade ..."

Die Bibliothek ist Teil des neuen Universitätscampus von Utrecht. Der Architekt wollte den Widerspruch zwischen offenen, zugänglichen Räumen für Studenten und Wissenschaftler und geschlossenen Bereichen zur Lagerung von Büchern und anderen lichtempfindlichen Dokumenten auflösen. „Die geschlossenen Raumvolumen des Magazins", so Arets, „hängen wie opake Wolken in der Luft, während die offene Konstruktion den Besuchern ein Gefühl von Geräumigkeit und Freiheit vermittelt." Die Glasfassaden wurden zum Schutz vor grellem Sonnenlichteinfall – und um den Bau „wie ein Haus im Wald" wirken zu lassen – im Siebdruckverfahren mit Pflanzenmotiven bedruckt. Die Haupttreppe führt zu einem Auditoriums- und Ausstellungsbereich und weiter zur eigentlichen Bibliothek im ersten Obergeschoss. Ein gebäudehoher Lichtschacht neben der zentralen Theke lässt Tageslicht herein. Ein Hof an der Ostseite des Gebäudes trennt die Bibliothek vom fünfstöckigen Parkhaus und sorgt dafür, dass auch die Räume hinter der Ostfassade natürlich beleuchtet werden. Die Glasfassaden des Parkhauses unterstreichen seine Zugehörigkeit zur Bibliothek. Kritiker bemängelten deren schwarze Geschlossenheit, worauf Arets erklärte, die UBU sei nicht nur ein Ort zum Bücherstudieren, sondern einer, „wo die Leute konzentriert arbeiten, sich aber auch mit anderen treffen können, ohne dass sie außer der Atmosphäre im Gebäude weitere Stimulanzien brauchen. Die wie schwebende Wolken wirkenden Buchmagazine unterteilen den Innenraum in verschiedene Zonen und sind über Treppen und Rampen miteinander verbunden. Die mit schwarzen, reliefierten Betonplatten verkleideten Magazinblöcke tragen die Lesesäle und sind zum Teil doppelt verglast."

Cette bibliothèque fait partie du nouveau a complexe de l'Université d'Utrecht. L'architecte a cherché à résoudre la contradiction inhérente entre le plan ouvert dont avaient besoin les étudiants et les chercheurs, et le plan fermé nécessaire à la conservation des livres et autres éléments des collections sensibles à la lumière. Selon Arets : « Les volumes fermés des réserves sont suspendus dans les airs comme des nuages opaques, et cependant la structure donne au visiteur une impression d'espace et de liberté. » Des motifs végétaux sérigraphiés sur les façades de verre ont été retenus comme thème décoratif général. Ils limitent la pénétration solaire et « génèrent une impression de bâtiment dans les bois ». L'escalier principal conduit à un auditorium et une galerie d'exposition puis à la bibliothèque proprement dite située au premier étage. Près de l'accueil central un grand volume vide traverse la totalité du bâtiment pour apporter la lumière naturelle. Sur le côté est, un patio sépare la bibliothèque du parking de cinq niveaux et facilite également la pénétration de la lumière. La façade de verre du parking souligne son appartenance au complexe. Aux critiques reprochant l'aspect sombre de ce projet Arets répond : « L'UBU ... est davantage qu'un endroit où les gens peuvent consulter des livres, c'est un lieu où ils peuvent travailler de manière concentrée, mais où ils peuvent aussi rencontrer d'autres gens, sans le besoin d'autres stimuli que l'atmosphère dont ce bâtiment irradie. Les réserves de livres, qui semblent flotter comme des nuages, divisent l'espace en zones et communiquent par des escaliers et des rampes. Les réserves en béton noirci sur lesquelles s'appuient les salles de lecture sont enchâssées dans une façade en partie à double vitrage ... »

The solution chosen by Arets for the library is a study in contrasts between black opacity and lightness. He speaks of the need to preserve the books as opposed to the desire of users for a feeling of freedom.

Bei dem Bibliotheksgebäude spielt Arets mit den Kontrasten zwischen Leichtigkeit und schwarzer Massivität. Der Architekt spricht von der Notwendigkeit, die Bücher zu konservieren und andererseits dem Nutzer räumliche Freiheit zu gewähren.

Pour cette bibliothèque universitaire, Arets a travaillé sur les contrastes entre la lumière et le noir opaque. Il parle d'opposition entre le besoin de protéger les livres et le désir de liberté des usagers.

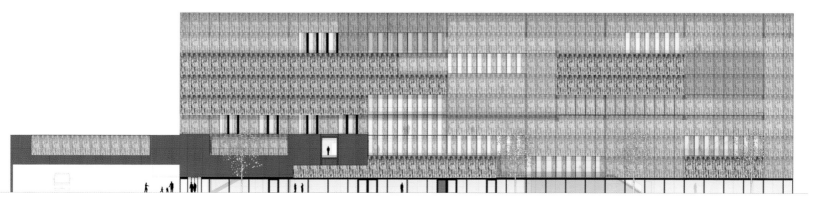

Although there has been some criticism of the darkness of the library, its open spaces and alternation of bright and black volumes give an unusual feeling to the interior spaces.

Zwar ist die Bibliothek aufgrund ihres dunklen Inneren kritisiert worden, ihre offenen Räume und das Wechselspiel von hellen und schwarzen Volumina sorgen aber dennoch für eine faszinierende Innenatmosphäre.

Si certaines critiques ont visé le caractère sombre de la bibliothèque, ses espaces ouverts et ses alternances de volumes noirs ou lumineux confèrent à son espace intérieur une atmosphère inhabituelle.

The persistent vegetal theme of the cladding or windows tie the otherwise modern architecture to the earth. The black patterning seen to the left might recall fossilized branches, as though the knowledge contained in the library, too, came from the depths of time.

Das Pflanzendekor der Fassadenelemente und Fenster erdet die moderne Architektur. Das schwarze Muster links im Bild erinnert an versteinerte Äste – so, als ob auch das in der Bibliothek gespeicherte Wissen aus den Tiefen des Lebens entsprungen sei.

Le thème végétal récurrent sur les habillages ou les fenêtres crée un lien entre cette architecture très moderne et la nature. Le motif noir à gauche évoque des branches fossiles, comme si les connaissances emmagasinées par la bibliothèque venaient des profondeurs de la vie.

COLOPHON STYLESUITE MAASTRICHT 2003 - 05

FLOOR AREA: 432 m²
CLIENT: M. A. C. V. Merkelbach/
Municipality of Maastricht
COST: €528 000

Located in the fashionable Stokstraat (35–37), Stylesuite is a multibrand fashion shop with an emphasis in this instance on Dolce & Gabbana. The architect faced the challenge of giving a sense of unity to an essentially fragmented space located in two different buildings on two floors. He chose to create a diagonal passageway that links four rooms horizontally, with an ample staircase linking the floors and allowing views of the full space of the shop. Existing walls were cleaned and painted white, while a homogeneous brown double wall was created to contain changing rooms, storage areas and a toilet space. The same brown tone is used for the floors, emphasizing the continuity of the newly fashioned space. "Twisted and mirrored" units of fiberglass with internal light sources are used for the display of the accessories and clothes. Daylight is let in to the shop through the existing windows and a rectangular glass element located in the courtyard behind the building. The architect appears to regret the use of "traditional mannequins," but he has succeeded not only in spatial terms in creating a unified architectural solution, but also in retail terms, providing more display areas within the overall volume of 1550 cubic meters.

Das an der schicken Stokstraat (35–37) gelegene Stylesuite ist ein mehrere Marken führendes Modegeschäft mit Schwerpunkt auf Dolce & Gabbana. Der Architekt sah sich der Schwierigkeit gegenüber, für einen im Grunde fragmentierten, auf zwei Gebäude und zwei Geschosse verteilten Raum ein organisches Ambiente zu schaffen. Er entschied sich für einen diagonalen Gang, der vier Räume horizontal miteinander verbindet, in Kombination mit einem geräumigen Treppenhaus zur Erschließung der Obergeschosse; von hier bieten sich Ausblicke in das gesamte Ladengeschäft. Vorhandene Wände wurden gereinigt und weiß verputzt und eine einheitlich braun gestrichene Doppelwand eingezogen, in der Umkleidekabinen, Lagerraum und Toiletten untergebracht sind. Derselbe Farbton wurde für die Böden verwendet und so der Zusammenhang der neu gestalteten Räume unterstrichen. „Verdrehte und verspiegelte", von innen beleuchtete Fiberglaselemente werden für die Präsentation von Accessoires und Kleidung genutzt. Tageslicht fällt durch bereits vorhandene Fenster sowie durch ein hinter dem Gebäude im Innenhof stehendes, rechteckiges Glaselement in den Laden. Der Architekt bedauert die Verwendung „herkömmlicher Schaufensterpuppen"; aber es gelang ihm, sowohl in räumlicher Hinsicht eine organische, architektonische Lösung zu finden als auch in geschäftlicher Hinsicht in dem Gesamtvolumen von 1550 m³ mehr Ausstellungsfläche zu schaffen.

Située dans l'élégante rue Stokstraat (35–37), Stylesuite est une boutique de mode multimarques qui met actuellement l'accent sur Dolce & Gabbana. L'architecte était confronté à la difficulté de conférer un sentiment d'unité à un espace très fragmenté découpé entre deux immeubles et deux niveaux. Il a décidé de créer un passage en diagonale qui relie horizontalement les quatre salles. Un généreux escalier relie les niveaux et permet une vision globale de la boutique. Les murs existants ont été peints en blanc et dans une double paroi de couleur marron se trouvent les cabines d'essayage, des rangements et des toilettes. La même tonalité brune est reprise sur les sols, confirmant ainsi la nouvelle unité des volumes (1550 m³). Des éléments en fibre de verre « en torsion et à effet de miroir » et éclairage interne servent à la présentation des accessoires et des vêtements. La lumière du jour vient des fenêtres existantes et d'un élément rectangulaire en verre implanté dans la cour derrière l'immeuble. L'architecte qui semble regretter les « mannequins traditionnels » a réussi à trouver une solution architecturale non seulement en termes de volumes mais en termes de vente puisqu'il offre d'avantage de possibilités de présentation des vêtements qu'auparavant.

Wiel Arets uses strong contrasts between light and dark in this fashion boutique, just as he did in the Utrecht University library, obviously to different ends and on a different scale.

Bei der Gestaltung dieser Modeboutique hat Wiel Arets – genau wie bei der Universitäts-bibliothek Utrecht – mit starken Hell-Dunkel-Kontrasten gearbeitet, allerdings mit einem anderen Ziel und in viel kleinerem Maßstab.

Dans cette boutique de mode comme dans la bibliothèque de l'Université d'Utrecht, Wiel Arets a mis en scène de puissants contrastes entre le lumineux et l'opaque, mais à une autre échelle et dans un but différent.

Clothes and accessories are presented like precious objects in display cases whose blackness links them to the floor and contrasts with the white upper reaches of the space.

Kleidungsstücke und Accessoires werden wie kostbare Objekte in Vitrinen präsentiert, die ebenso schwarz sind wie der Fußboden – im Kontrast zur weißen oberen Hälfte des Raums.

Les vêtements et les accessoires sont présentés comme des objets précieux dans des casiers dont la noirceur étudiée rappelle celle du sol et contraste avec la blancheur éclatante de la partie haute de la boutique.

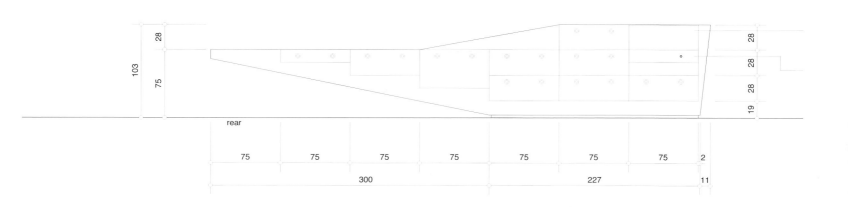

2

ERICK VAN EGERAAT

**(EEA) ERICK VAN EGERAAT
ASSOCIATED ARCHITECTS**
Calandstraat 23
3016 CA Rotterdam

Tel: +31 10 4 36 96 86
Fax: +31 10 4 36 95 73
e-mail: eea@eea-architects.com
Web: www.eea-architects.com

One of the most promising architects of his generation, **ERICK VAN EGERAAT** was born in 1956 in Amsterdam. He created Mecanoo architecten with Henk Döll, Chris de Weijer and Francine Houben in Delft in 1983. Their work included large housing projects, such as the Herdenkingsplein in Maastricht (1990–92), and smaller-scale projects, such as their 1990 Boompjes Pavilion, a cantilevered structure overlooking the harbor of Rotterdam, close to the new Erasmus Bridge, or a private house in Rotterdam (1989–91). He left Mecanoo in 1995 with 17 members of the staff and created Erick van Egeraat Associated Architects. He declared his intention to go towards a "warm, inviting architecture," which he calls "Modern Baroque" as opposed to a more neo-modern style favored by Mecanoo. Though the firm is based in Rotterdam, Erick van Egeraat has developed numerous projects in eastern Europe and Russia. Recent work of the firm aside from the two projects published here includes: Extension ING office, Paulay Ede utca, Budapest (1997); Liget Center, Dózsa György út 84 a, Budapest (2001); Luxury apartments Mauritskade, Amsterdam (2002); Villa Bianca, Prague (2003); and the ING Head Office at Dózsa György út 84 b, Budapest (2004). He has also made an interesting proposal for a series of five residential towers for a site in Moscow located in the Yakimanka area, across from the New Tretyakov Museum, an institution that has one of the best collections of Russian avant-garde painting. Seizing on this fact, Van Egeraat decided that each of the towers would refer to a work by the artists Vasily Kandinsky, Aleksandr Rodchenko, Lyubov Popova, Kazimir Malevich, and Alexandra Exter.

POPSTAGE
BREDA
1996-2002

FLOOR AREA: 1600 m²
CLIENT: City of Breda
COST: €3.5 million

The Popstage consists of a concert hall for 650 people and a café in an existing officers' canteen for 150 people. Part of an urban development scheme conceived by OMA in the so-called Chassée-terrein area of Breda, a former military base, the Popstage is located in the southwest corner of the site and includes 720 m² of new construction. Shaped like "a voluptuous seashell adjoining the existing structure," the new building is clearly visible from the 'entertainment district' of the city. Nearby residences required the use of a double dome with an air gap of one meter between the shells to reduce noise problems from the planned concerts. The exterior shell is a "hybrid structure of steel and concrete that for acoustic reasons is covered by 100 mm of poured concrete and a pre-oxidized copper skin." The metaphor of a closed shell was extended to the entrance options chosen by the architect. A three by four meter steel frame door conceived like that of a ferryboat closes and leaves little if any trace of an opening in the exterior shell of the Popstage. Because its shape is the result of careful study of the requirements of the project, the blob-like appearance of the Popstage is not a real indication of a purely computer-driven design. Erick van Egeraat was one of the first to experiment with the juxtaposition of old architecture with contemporary, organic intrusions in his Head Offices for ING and NNH (Andrássy út Budapest, 1994), where he added the "Whale," a conference room made out of 26 laminated timber frames using techniques akin to shipbuilding, to an 1882 Italianate building. The Popstage builds on this concept in a different context.

Bei der Popstage handelt es sich um den Umbau einer früheren Offiziersmesse in eine Konzerthalle für 650 Zuhörer mit zugehörigem Café für 150 Besucher. Die Popbühne ist Teil eines von OMA entwickelten Masterplans für das Chassé-Terrain, ein ehemaliges Kasernengelände in Breda. Der Altbau liegt in der Südwestecke des Plangebiets und wurde um 720 m² erweitert. Der Neubauteil erinnert an eine kurvenreiche Meeresmuschel und ist vom Zentrum der Stadt aus gut zu sehen. Van Egeraat schuf eine Doppelkuppel mit einer Lücke von einem Meter zwischen den Schalen, um die Lärmemission von den Popkonzerten zum Schutz der benachbarten Wohnbebauung zu minimieren. Die äußere Schale ist eine „Hybridform aus Stahl und Beton, die aus akustischen Gründen mit einer 100 mm dicken Ortbetonschicht und voroxidiertem Kupferblech gedeckt ist". Die

Metapher der geschlossenen Muschelschale wandte der Architekt auch auf die Eingangssituation an: Die 3 x 4 m große stahlgerahmte Tür wirkt offen wie das geöffnete „Maul" eines Fährschiffs, hinterlässt in geschlossenem Zustand aber kaum eine Spur in der Fassade der Popstage. Da sich deren Form in enger Verbindung mit dem vorgegebenen Raumprogramm ergab, ist sie kein richtiges Beispiel für computergestütztes Entwerfen. Erick van Egeraat war einer der Ersten, der mit der Kombination von Altbauten und neuen organischen Anbauten experimentierte, z. B. bei seinen ING- und NNH-Projekten in Budapest (1994), wo er in Anlehnung an den Schiffsbau aus 26 Schichtholzbögen einen „Walfisch" schuf, der auf einem 1882 im italienischen Stil erbauten Gebäude einen Konferenzraum beherbergt. Die Popstage greift dieses Konzept in einem anderen Kontext auf.

Cette Popstage regroupe une salle de concerts pop de 650 places et un café de 150 places aménagé dans un ancien mess d'officiers. Faisant partie du programme de développement conçu par OMA pour la zone de Chassée-Terrein à Breda, ancienne base militaire, la Popstage est située à l'angle sud-ouest du site et comprend 750 m² de construction neuve. En forme de « voluptueux coquillage collé à une construction existante », ce nouveau bâtiment est visible du quartier commercial de la ville. La présence de logements à proximité a demandé la pose d'une double coque dont chaque partie est séparée par un mètre d'air pour réduire les nuisances sonores des concerts. La coque extérieure est une « structure hybride d'acier et de béton qui, pour des raisons acoustiques, est recouverte de 100 mm de béton projeté et d'une peau de cuivre prépatiné ». La métaphore de la coquille fermée se retrouve dans les options d'entrée choisies par l'architecte. Un portail de 3 x 4 m conçu comme la porte d'un ferry-boat disparaît lorsqu'il se referme sur la structure. L'aspect de *blob* de ce projet résulte d'une étude approfondie des contraintes et non d'une conception purement informatisée. Erick van Egeraat a très tôt expérimenté la juxtaposition d'architectures anciennes et contemporaines comme dans les sièges de ING et de NNH (Andrassy ut, Budapest, 1994) où il avait créé la « Baleine », salle de conférence construite comme un bateau à partir de 26 cadres de bois lamellé sur un bâtiment italianisant datant de 1882. La Popstage développe ce concept dans un contexte différent.

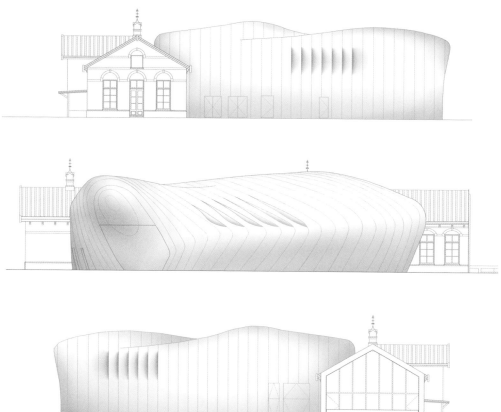

The nearly anthropomorphic folds of the Popstage bring to mind Van Egeraat's earlier headquarters for ING & NNH at Andrássy út in Budapest with its laminated-wood "Whale" conference room.

Die fast anthropomorphe Faltung der Popstage erinnert an Van Egeraats Zentrale der ING & NNH-Bank in Budapest mit ihrem „Walfisch", einem Konferenzraum aus Schichtholz.

Les plis quasi anthropomorphiques de la Popstage font penser au siège d'ING et de NNH Andrassy ut à Budapest de Van Egeraat célèbre pour sa salle de réunion en bois lamellé-collé appelée « la baleine ».

The unusual shape of the exterior of the building makes sense as seen from within with the audience space wrapping around the rock stage seen below.

Die ungewöhnliche Form des Gebäudes wird erst im Innern verständlich, wo der Zuschauerraum das tief liegende Rockkonzertpodium umgibt.

Ci-dessous, la forme curieuse du bâtiment prend tout son sens à l'intérieur dans l'enveloppement de la scène par la salle.

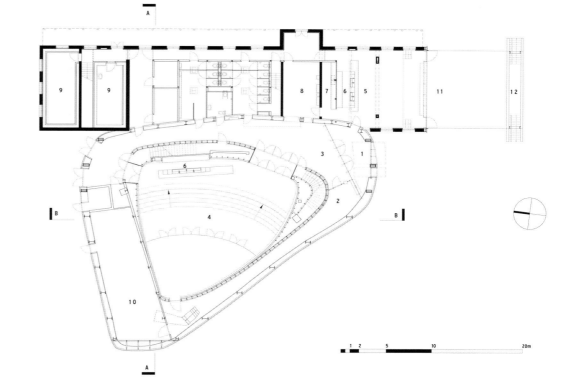

CITY HALL
ALPHEN AAN DEN RIJN
1997-2002

FLOOR AREA: 25 000 m²
CLIENT: City of Alphen aan den Rijn
COST: €25 million

This new city hall building with a floor area of 25 000 m² and a garage for 240 cars was completed in December 2002. It has 5.5 levels above ground and an 18-meter-high atrium. The project was part of an ambitious master plan conceived by the city with the developer MAB, Erick van Egeraat Associated Architects and Kraaijvanger · Urbis. Despite its existing amenities, Alphen aan den Rijn did not have a real city center and the project aimed to develop just that with a new theater/cinema complex, shops, cafés and restaurants, housing, offices, the City Hall, 1000 parking spaces, parking for 600 bicycles and a new public square on the Old Rhine. MAB developed the retail area, and the City Council was responsible for its own offices, which were intended to have a "transparent, open and inviting" appearance. A transparent glass curtain wall is one way Erick van Egeraat responded to this request. All public facilities are located on the ground floor and the council hall is spectacularly cantilevered over the entrance. The architect sought to modulate the height of the building according to the neighboring urban scale, raising it, for example, on the side of Roaul Wallenberg Square and lowering opposite residential buildings. These variations together with the wrap-around skin give the city hall building a decidedly modern appearance, which led to the project being selected for exhibition at the 2004 Venice Architecture Biennale. Although EEA does not emphasize computer-driven designs as much as some Dutch offices, the city hall building was the object of a case study by students in the socalled Blob Technology Group at the Faculty of Architecture of the Delft Technical University. As Erick van Egeraat says, "it can be seen as a contemporary beacon, reflecting the growing community's image."

Die Stadthalle mit einer Geschossfläche von 25 000 m² und Stellplätzen für 240 Autos wurde im Dezember 2002 fertig gestellt. Sie umfasst 5,5 Geschosse über Straßenniveau und ein 18 m hohes Atrium. Das Bauvorhaben gehört zu einem von der Stadt zusammen mit dem Investor MAB und den Architekturbüros Erick van Egeraat Associated Architects und Kraaijvanger · Urbis geplanten ehrgeizigen Stadtentwicklungsprojekt. Alphen aan den Rijn besaß kein richtiges Stadtzentrum und genau das sollte gebaut werden – mit einem neuen Theater- und Kinogebäude, Läden, Gastronomie, Wohnungen, Büros, Stadthalle, Stellplätzen für 1000 Autos und 600 Fahrräder sowie einem neuen Stadtplatz am Ufer des Altrheins. MAB entwickelte das Einkaufszentrum, während der Stadtrat für seine eigenen Räume verantwortlich war, die „transparent, offen und einladend" sein sollten. Erick van Egeraat ging mit einer transparenten Glasvorhangfassade auf diesen Wunsch ein. Alle öffentlichen Bereiche befinden sich im Erdgeschoss; der Sitzungssaal des

Stadtrats kragt höchst eindrucksvoll über dem Haupteingang aus. Der Architekt reagierte mit einer Staffelung der Gebäudehöhe auf den umliegenden Bestand, so dass der Bau zum Raoul-Wallenberg-Platz höher und zum Wohnviertel auf der anderen Seite niedriger ist. Diese Modulierung und die Gebäudehülle verleihen der Stadthalle ein entschieden modernes Erscheinungsbild, weshalb der Entwurf auch zur Ausstellung auf der Architekturbiennale 2004 in Venedig ausgewählt wurde. Obwohl EEA das computergenerierte Entwerfen nicht in dem Maß betreibt wie andere niederländische Büros, war die Stadthalle Gegenstand einer Fallstudie der so genannten Blob Technology Group von Studenten an der Architekturfakultät der TU Delft. „Sie kann als zeitgenössischer Leuchtturm aufgefasst werden", so Erick van Egeraat, „der das Image der wachsenden Stadt reflektiert."

Ce nouvel hôtel de ville de 25 000 m² utiles complété par un garage pour 240 véhicules a été achevé en décembre 2002. Il comprend cinq niveaux et demi au-dessus du sol et un atrium de 18 m de haut. Le projet fait partie d'un ambitieux plan directeur établi par la ville et le promoteur MAB, Erick van Egeraat Associated Architects et Kraaijvanger · Urbis. Malgré son développement, la ville ne possédait pas encore de vrai centre, qui était justement l'objectif de ce projet prévoyant la création d'un complexe de cinémas/théâtre, boutiques, cafés, restaurants, logements, bureaux, l'hôtel de ville, 1000 places de parking pour voitures, 600 pour vélos et une nouvelle place publique donnant sur le Vieux Rhin. MAB a traité les parties commerciales et le conseil municipal s'est chargé de ses bureaux qui devaient présenter un aspect « transparent, ouvert et convivial ». Le mur-rideau transparent en vert est un des moyens choisis par Erick van Egeraat pour répondre à cette demande. Tous les équipements ouverts au public sont situés au rez-de-chaussée et la salle du conseil se développe spectaculairement en porte-à-faux au-dessus de l'entrée. L'architecte a cherché à moduler la hauteur de l'immeuble par rapport à l'échelle urbaine en l'élevant du côté de la place Raul Wallenberg et en l'abaissant face à des immeubles de logement. Ces variations et la peau enveloppante donnent à l'ensemble une apparence décidément moderne qui a fait sélectionner ce projet pour la Biennale d'architecture de Venise en 2004. Bien que EEA ne soit pas aussi attaché à la conception assistée par ordinateur que d'autres agences néerlandaises, cette réalisation a été l'objet d'une étude de cas du Blob Technology Group de la faculté d'architecture de l'Université de technologie de Delft. Comme le fait remarquer Erick van Egeraat, « il peut être considéré comme un signal contemporain, qui reflète l'image d'une communauté en développement ».

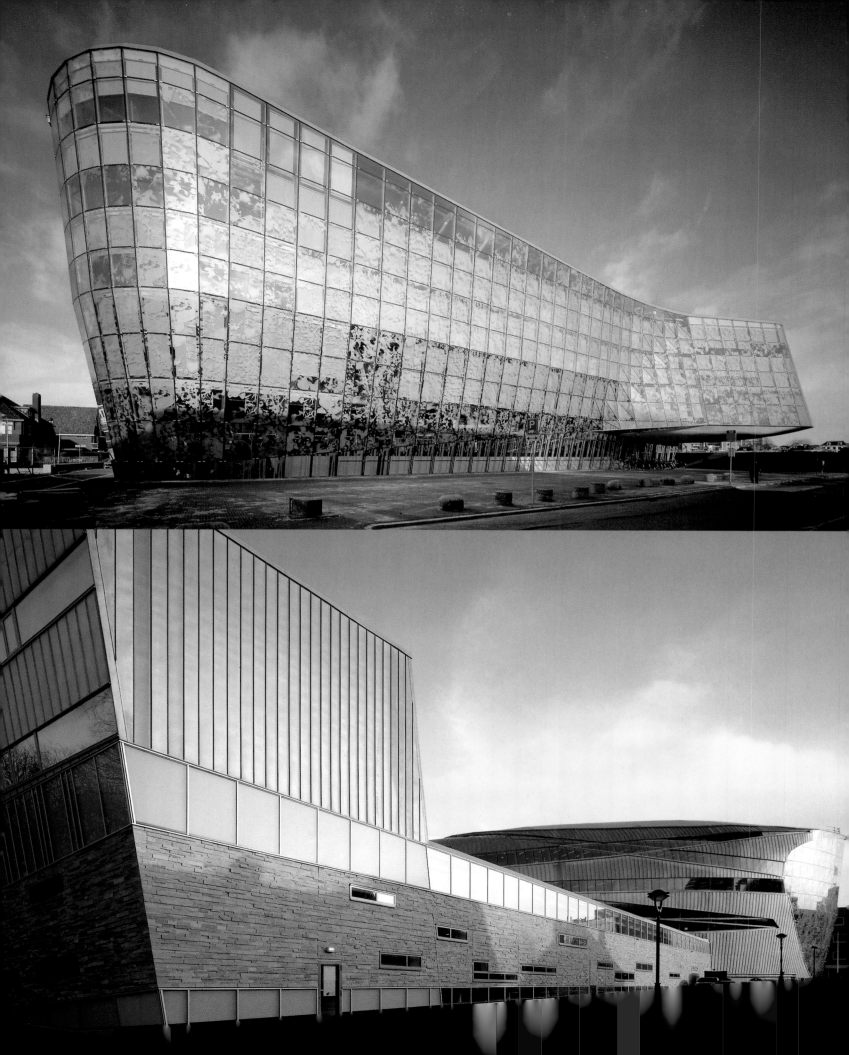

A central feature of the city hall is its five-level, 18-meter-high atrium. Resolved with an almost industrial palette of materials and Piranesian gestures, such as the suspended walkways, the atrium gives the whole building a feeling of spatial surprise.

Ein zentrales Element der Stadthalle ist das fünfstöckige, 18 m hohe Atrium. Mit seiner industriell anmutenden Materialpalette und den an Piranesi erinnernden Elementen wie den Hängebrücken verleiht das Atrium dem gesamten Gebäude ein überraschendes Raumgefühl.

L'élément central de l'hôtel de ville est un atrium de 18 m et cinq niveaux de haut. Geste piranésien traité dans une palette de matériaux quasi industriels comme dans le cas des passerelles suspendues, il crée un sentiment de surprise indéniable.

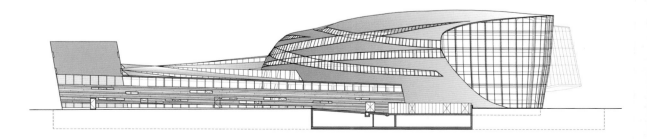

A plan of the building shows that it has more than an unusual façade—the functions of the city hall are laid out within the overall pod-like design.

Der Grundriss bestätigt, dass der Bau mehr als nur eine ungewöhnliche Fassade bietet. Die Funktionen der Stadthalle sind in das Design wie in eine Hülse eingepasst.

Le plan de l'immeuble montre que sa façade étonnante n'est pas sa seule spécificité : les fonctions municipales se répartissent selon un plan en *pod*.

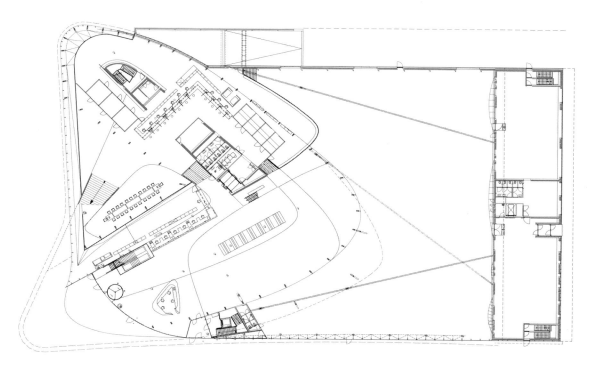

3

HERMAN HERTZBERGER

ARCHITECTUURSTUDIO HERMAN HERTZBERGER AMSTERDAM
Gerard Doustraat 220
1073 XB Amsterdam

Tel: +31 20 6 76 58 88
Fax: +31 20 6 73 55 10
e-mail: office@hertzberger.nl
Web: www.hertzberger.nl

Born in Amsterdam in 1932, **HERMAN HERTZBERGER** studied at the Technical University of Delft, from which he graduated in 1958. He opened his own office in 1958. Editor of *Forum* magazine with Aldo van Eyck from 1959 to 1963, he was a Professor at the Technical University of Delft from 1970 to 1999. He was Chairman of the Berlage Institute, Amsterdam, from 1990 to 1995, where Wiel Arets succeeded him. His built work includes eight experimental houses, Gebbenlaan, Delft (1969–70); Vredenburg Music Center, Utrecht (1973–78); Kindergarten/Primary School "De Evenaar," Amsterdam (1984–86); Office building for the Ministry of Social Welfare and Employment, The Hague (1979–90); Spui Theater Center, The Hague (1986–93); Chassé Theater, Breda (1992–95); Markant Theater, Uden (1993–96); Urban design/master plan for Stralauer Halbinsel, Berlin (1994–98); residential buildings, "Growing Houses," Hans Lodeizenstraat, Jan Hanlostraat, Hans Andreusstraat, Lucebertstraat, Almere (1998–2002); "Il Fiore" Office Building, Avenue Céramique, Maastricht (1998–2002); and Titaan Secondary School, Hoorn (1999–2004). Current work includes the DWR office building, Amsterdam; Faculty of Natural Sciences, Mathematics and Information Technology of the University of Amsterdam, Watergraafsmeer Science Park, Amsterdam; and Supervision of the urban design for the Veersche Poort residential area, Middelburg.

WATERVILLA
MIDDELBURG
1998 - 2002

FLOOR AREA: 160 m²
CLIENT: Woongoed Middelburg, Middelburg
COST: €420 000

Herman Hertzberger first designed a nearly cylindrical house intended to float on the water in 1986, but it was only more recently that he had the opportunity to build a prototype intended for the Veersche Poort district of Middelburg, where he supervises urban planning. The house floats on six interconnected two-meter-long, ten-millimeter-thick steel offshore pipes. Intended for long immersion, these pipes require little or no maintenance and can be used for storage if required. The practical aspect expressed in the flotation system is carried through in the rest of the design, which is made from a steel skeleton with low-maintenance exterior and interior metallic façades. The built prototype has a gross floor area of 160 m², but the design allows for numerous variations. Three floors with external terraces can be outfitted as the owner wishes, with the living room, for example, located on any floor. Combined with the very idea of a floating house, the open design fosters a feeling of freedom and independence usually not found in a residence. As the architect points out, it is easy to turn the house so that it benefits from the best solar exposure, for example. Although the Netherlands are obviously a choice location for housing intended for the water, the flexibility and robustness of this design make it potentially much more interesting than any traditional house. Perhaps better known for large housing complexes or theaters than for such individual prototypes, Herman Hertzberger has put his considerable knowledge to good use with the Watervilla.

Schon 1986 hatte Herman Hertzberger ein beinahe zylindrisches Hausboot entworfen, aber erst vor einigen Jahren bekam er die Chance, für das Veersche Hafengebiet der Stadt Middelburg (deren städtebaulicher Supervisor er ist) einen Prototyp zu bauen. Das Haus schwimmt auf sechs miteinander verbundenen, 2 m langen Stahlrohren mit 10 mm dicker Wandung, die speziell zur Langzeitverwendung unter Wasser produziert werden und daher keine oder nur wenig Instandhaltung erfordern; falls nötig, kann man sie auch als Stauräume nutzen. Der Architekt übertrug die praktischen Aspekte dieses Pontonsystems auch auf das Haus selbst, das aus einem Stahlgerüst mit pflegeleichter Metallverkleidung innen wie außen besteht. Der Prototyp hat eine Bruttogeschossfläche von 160 m²; der Entwurf ermöglicht aber auch zahlreiche Varianten. Drei Geschosse mit Außenterrassen lassen sich ganz nach Wunsch des Besitzers einteilen und ausstatten, das

Wohnzimmer kann z. B. auf jeder Etage eingerichtet werden. Zusätzlich zum Hausboot-Konzept an sich vermittelt auch das offene Interieur ein Gefühl der Unabhängigkeit, das ein normales, bodenständiges Haus nicht bietet. Der Architekt wies darauf hin, dass sein Pontonhaus mühelos gedreht werden kann, damit es z. B. optimal von der Sonneneinstrahlung profitiert. Natürlich sind die Niederlande das Land der Wahl für den Bau von „wassergängigen" Häusern, die Flexibilität und Robustheit dieses Exemplars machen es aber ohnehin viel interessanter als ein traditionelles Haus. Zwar ist Hertzberger bekannter für seine großen Wohnsiedlungen oder Theater als für derartige kleine Entwürfe, er hat sein umfangreiches Wissen aber beim Entwurf dieser Wasservilla gut umgesetzt.

Herman Hertzberger avait conçu en 1986 une maison quasi cylindrique qui devait flotter sur l'eau, mais ce n'est que récemment qu'il a eu l'opportunité de construire un prototype pour le quartier du Veersche Poort à Middelburg dont il supervise l'urbanisme. La maison flotte sur six sections interconnectées de deux mètres de long fabriquées à partir d'une conduite sous-marine en acier épais de 10 mm. Conçus pour une immersion permanente, ces tuyaux ne nécessitent que peu ou pas de maintenance et peuvent même servir de volume de stockage si nécessaire. L'aspect pratique de ce système de flottaison se retrouve dans le reste du projet qui fait appel à une structure en acier à façades métalliques intérieures et extérieures à maintenance réduite. Le prototype offre une surface totale de 160 m², mais le projet permet de nombreuses variantes. Trois niveaux à terrasses extérieures peuvent être mis en place selon les souhaits du propriétaire, le séjour pouvant se trouver à n'importe quel niveau. Ajoutée à l'idée d'une maison flottante, la conception ouverte fait naître un sentiment de liberté et d'indépendance que l'on ne trouve généralement pas dans une maison privée. Comme le fait remarquer l'architecte, il est facile d'orienter la maison en fonction de la meilleure exposition solaire, par exemple. Bien que les Pays-Bas soient un terrain d'expérimentation favorable à des maisons sur l'eau, la souplesse et la robustesse de ce projet lui donnent un intérêt qui dépasse celui des conceptions traditionnelles. Plus connu pour ses grands complexes de logements et ses théâtres que ses prototypes, Herman Hertzberger a mobilisé sa considérable expérience dans cette « villa d'eau ».

Although it is closely linked to the earth,
the Watervilla has something of a ship about
it, albeit a ship with no discernable prow or
stern.

Obwohl mit dem Festland verbunden,
erinnert die „Wasservilla" auch an ein Schiff,
allerdings eines ohne ausgeprägten Bug
oder erkennbares Heck.

Bien que reliée au sol, la Watervilla fait penser
à un bateau dont on ne saurait où se trouvent
la proue et la poupe.

With its alternation of closed and open façades, the Watervilla is intended to be turned according to sun conditions, as can be seen in the drawings below.

Mit ihrem Wechsel von offenen und geschlossenen Fassadenflächen kann die „Wasservilla" je nach Sonnenstand gedreht werden.

Avec son alternance de façades ouvertes et fermées, la Watervilla s'oriente en fonction du soleil, comme le montre le schéma ci-dessous.

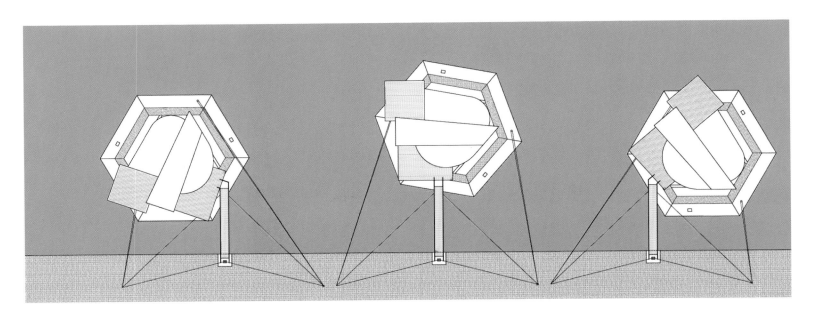

CODA
CULTURAL CENTER
APELDOORN
1999 - 2004

FLOOR AREA: 9000 m²
CLIENT: City of Apeldoorn
COST: €16.2 million

This 9000 m² facility is a multiple-use building containing two museums, an extension to the adjoining public library, and the municipal archives, with a reading room, offices, study spaces, and a restaurant. The eighth most populous city of the Netherlands, with about 150 000 inhabitants, Apeldoorn is located 90 kilometers east of Amsterdam. Herman Hertzberger has had a long relationship with the city since he built an office building for the Centraal Beheer insurance company there in 1973. Made of precast concrete, this office building is cited as an example of flexibility since its small spatial units can be strung together in various ways, allowing for the company to change and adapt over time. The name CODA is an acronym for Culture Under One Roof Apeldoorn in Dutch (Cultuur Onder Dak Apeldoorn). "It is a container-like building," as Herman Hertzberger puts it, "in which the expression comes from within." All of the occupants face outwards and are visible through the glass skin of the building. By way of contrast, the lower volume, likened by the architects to a "transparent display case," is topped by a "hermetically sealed box housing the municipal archives." With the exception of this black concrete slab, the rest of the structure places an obvious emphasis on openness, even inside. Despite the ability of each organization to close itself off to some extent, voids connect the spaces, underlining their shared dependency on the public. Echoing the theme of flexibility that is implied by the overall transparency of the complex, the museum space with its curved roof is sunken in good part below a courtyard. Together with the steps, this roof forms a public urban space where in the summer events take place.

Dieser Mehrzweckbau mit 9000 m² Geschossfläche beherbergt zwei Museen, eine Zweigstelle der Stadtbibliothek, das Stadtarchiv, Lesesaal, Büros, Seminarräume und ein Restaurant. Apeldoorn, mit rund 150 000 Einwohnern die achtgrößte Stadt der Niederlande, liegt 90 km östlich von Amsterdam. Herman Hertzberger ist bereits mit der Stadt verbunden, seit er dort 1973 ein Bürogebäude für die Centraal-Beheer-Versicherung realisierte, das als beispielhaft flexibel gilt, weil sich seine kleinen Raumeinheiten auf unterschiedlichste Weise kombinieren lassen und damit Veränderungen dem Betrieb angepasst werden können. Das Akronym CODA steht für Cultuur Onder Dak Apeldoorn (Kultur unter [einem] Dach Apeldoorn). „Es ist eine Art Container", erklärt Herman Hertzberger, „dessen Ausdruckskraft von innen kommt." Alle Mitarbeiter haben Sichtkontakt zur Außenwelt und sind selbst durch die Glasfassaden von außen zu sehen. Der Sockelbau-

körper – den die Architekten mit einem „transparenten Schaukasten" verglichen – wird bekrönt vom „hermetisch verschlossenen Kasten des Stadtarchivs". Mit Ausnahme dieses schwarzen Betonriegels ist das Gebäude äußerst offen und transparent, auch im Innern. Die einzelnen Organisationen können sich zwar bis zu einem gewissen Grad voneinander abgrenzen, die verbindenden Lufträume unterstreichen aber ihre gemeinsame Abhängigkeit von der Öffentlichkeit. Die Durchlässigkeit und Flexibilität des Gebäudes kommen auch im Museumsbereich zum Tragen, dessen Räume zu einem guten Teil unter einem Innenhof liegen. Das geschwungene Dach des Museums und der Treppenaufgang zum Dach bilden einen öffentlichen Raum, der im Sommer für Veranstaltungen genutzt wird.

Ce bâtiment public de 9000 m² est un immeuble à plusieurs fonctions contenant deux musées, une extension de la bibliothèque publique voisine, les archives municipales, une salle de conférence, des bureaux, des espaces de recherche et un restaurant. Huitième ville néerlandaise, comptant environ 150 000 habitants, Apeldoorn est située à 90 km à l'ouest d'Amsterdam. Herman Hertzberger entretient une relation de longue date avec elle puisqu'il y avait construit un immeuble de bureaux pour la compagnie d'assurance Centraal Beheer en 1973. En béton préfabriqué, cet immeuble est resté exemplaire pour sa flexibilité puisque ses petites unités spatiales peuvent s'accoler de façons diverses permettant à l'entreprise d'évoluer avec le temps. Le nom de CODA est un acronyme pour « Culture sous un même toit », en néerlandais. « C'est un immeuble-conteneur », explique Hertzberger, « dans lequel l'expression vient de l'intérieur. » Toutes les parties sont orientées vers l'extérieur et visibles à travers la peau de verre de la façade. Par contraste, le volume inférieur, comparé par l'architecte à une « vitrine transparente » est surmonté d'une « boîte hermétiquement scellée contenant les archives municipales ». À l'exception de cette dalle de béton noir, le reste de la structure met l'accent fermement sur l'ouverture, y compris à l'intérieur. Malgré la tendance de chaque organisme présent à se refermer sur lui-même, des vides connectent les espaces pour souligner leur interdépendance par rapport au public. En écho au thème de la flexibilité impliqué par la transparence d'ensemble, l'espace muséal à toiture incurvée se retrouve pour sa plus grande partie sous une cour. Avec les escaliers, ce toit constitue un nouvel espace public où se déroulent des manifestations en été.

A curved roof in a courtyard serves as an alternative public space, emphasizing the continuity of the apparently disparate functions of the complex.

Das geschwungene Dach über dem Museum bildet einen Innenhof, der als öffentlicher Platz zugänglich ist und die Kontinuität der nur scheinbar sehr verschiedenen Funktionen innerhalb des Komplexes betont.

Une toiture incurvée dans une cour fait office de place publique alternative et met en évidence la continuité des fonctions apparemment disparates du complexe.

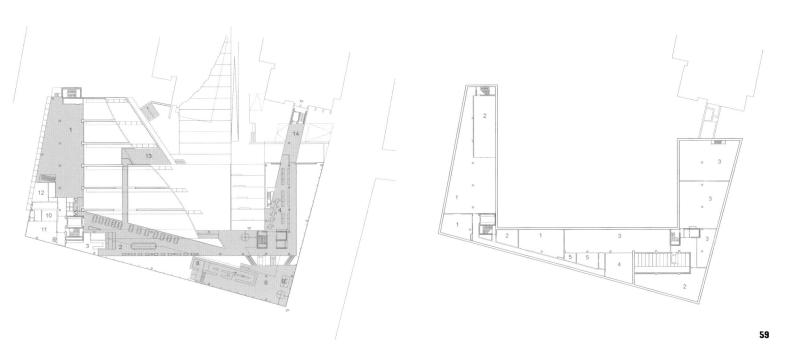

Bright, open spaces and inclined ramps linking levels again emphasize internal continuity despite the use of the CODA Center by various organizations.

Helle, offene Räume und Verbindungsrampen zwischen den Geschossen sorgen für räumliche Kontinuität, obwohl das CODA-Kulturzentrum von verschiedenen Organisationen genutzt wird.

Des espaces ouverts et lumineux et des rampes inclinées reliant les étages font ressortir la continuité spatiale même si le Centre CODA est utilisé par des organisations très diverses.

Overhead bridges, banks of steps and large, column-free spaces give a feeling of free circulation in these interior images.

Brückenstege, breite Treppen und große stützenfreie Räume vermitteln auf diesen Innenansichten ein Gefühl von freier Bewegung.

Des passerelles suspendues, des volées de marches et de vastes espaces sans la moindre colonne créent un sentiment de liberté de circulation.

MEYER EN VAN SCHOOTEN

#4

**MEYER EN VAN SCHOOTEN
ARCHITECTEN BV**
Pilotenstraat 35
1059 CH Amsterdam

Tel: +31 20 5 31 98 00
Fax: +31 20 5 31 98 01
e-mail: i.oosterheerd
@meyer-vanschooten.nl
Web: www.meyer-vanschooten.nl/

ROBERTO MEYER was born in 1959 in Bogotá, Colombia, while **JEROEN VAN SCHOOTEN** was born in Nieuwer Amstel in 1960. They were both educated at the HTS Architecture, Utrecht, and the Academies of Architecture in Amsterdam and Arnhem. They created their firm, Meyer en Van Schooten Architecten BV, in Amsterdam in 1984. Their work includes housing in Enschede, Apeldoorn, Amsterdam, Rotterdam, Zaandam, and Arnhem. They have also built a number of bridges in IJburg, Amsterdam (1998). Their recent work includes: 60 apartments, Geuzenbaan, Amsterdam; Blok 3, Central Library/30 apartments/offices/shops, Almere; 150 apartments + parking, Verolme terrain, Alblasserdam; 52 apartments in block 11 and 78 apartments in block 14b Gershwin, south axis, Amsterdam; and the 160 apartment Veranda complex in Rotterdam. Their ING Group Headquarters, Amsterdam (1998–2002) won several awards, including the 2002 Netherlands Steel Prize (Nationale Staalprijs 2002) and the Aluminum Architecture Award 2003 (Nederlandse Aluminium Award Architectuur 2003). They were selected in December 2003 to design the new Rotterdam Central Station (with Benthem Crouwel Architekten and West 8).

SHOEBALOO
AMSTERDAM
2002 · 03

FLOOR AREA: 190 m^2
CLIENT: H. Streim/SHOEBALOO BV, Amsterdam
COST: €500 000

With just 190 m^2 of usable floor space, the Shoebaloo shop in Amsterdam is much smaller than most other projects undertaken by Meyer en Van Schooten. Shoebaloo first opened its P. C. Hooftstraat store twelve years ago with an interior by the Czech designer Bořek Šípek. In this fashionable shopping area, Meyer en Van Schooten chose to create an understated façade with one-way glass that becomes transparent only when light is shone behind it. Shoes displayed in the window thus appear to hover in space when spotlights are directed on them. The more theatrical architectural event occurs when visitors come inside. Vacuum-molded translucent polyacrylic plastic was used for the ceiling and wall-mounted shelving, with niches for the display of shoes, all of which is in a 19th-century building. The floor is covered in glass set on more of the acrylic panels. Glossy white seats, a cash desk and display cases for accessories are "Barbarella-style and egg-shaped," according to the architects. One of the most unusual aspects of the design has to do with the lighting. Behind the plastic shell are 540 fluorescent bulbs, allowing either for a set lighting pattern or a slowly changing array of colors controlled by computer. A second Shoebaloo store was designed by the architects for Rotterdam. By evoking "Barbarella," the architects give some indication of the period of recent design history they are interested in, but here they have interpreted the theme using very contemporary technology and taste.

Mit gerade einmal 190 m^2 Nutzfläche ist das Schuhgeschäft Shoebaloo in Amsterdam viel kleiner als die meisten der von Meyer en Van Schooten ausgeführten Projekte. Zwölf Jahre zuvor hatte Shoebaloo den Laden in der P. C. Hooftstraat mit einer Inneneinrichtung des tschechischen Designers Bořek Šípek eröffnet. Angesichts der noblen Geschäftslage entschieden sich Meyer en Van Schooten für eine zurückhaltende Fassade aus Spiegelglas, das erst dann transparent wird, wenn man es von hinten beleuchtet. Sobald Scheinwerfer auf sie gerichtet werden, scheinen die im Fenster ausgestellten Schuhe deshalb im Raum zu schweben. Der theatralischere architektonische Effekt tritt jedoch ein, wenn man das Geschäft betritt. Im Vakuum geformtes transluzentes Polyacryl wurde für die Decken- und Wandverkleidungen verwendet und mit Nischen für die Auslagen versehen – all dies in einem Gebäude aus dem 19. Jahrhundert. Der Fußboden

ist mit Glas über den gleichen Polyacrylpaneelen ausgelegt. Glänzend weiße Sessel, eine Kassentheke und Vitrinen für Accessoires sind nach Aussage der Architekten im „Barbarella-Stil und eiförmig" gestaltet. Einer der ungewöhnlichsten Aspekte des Entwurfs hängt mit der Beleuchtung zusammen. Mit 540 Leuchtstoff-röhren hinter den Polyacrylwänden und -decken lässt sich entweder eine gleich-mäßige Beleuchtung oder – computergesteuert – ein langsam wechselndes Licht-spektrum erzeugen. Mit der „Barbarella"-Anspielung verweisen die Architekten auf eine Periode der jüngeren Designgeschichte, der sie zugeneigt sind. Hier haben sie das Thema mit modernster Technik und nach neuestem Geschmack interpretiert. In Rotterdam gestalteten die Architekten eine zweite Shoebaloo-Boutique.

Avec ses 190 m^2 à peine de surface au sol utile, la boutique Shoebaloo à Amsterdam est une réalisation beaucoup plus petite que la plupart des projets entrepris par Meyer en Van Schooten. Shoebaloo y avait ouvert il y a douze ans une boutique aménagée par le designer tchèque Bořek Šípek. Dans ce quartier à la mode, Meyer en Van Schooten ont opté pour une façade discrète en verre traité qui ne devient transparent que lorsque l'intérieur de la vitrine est illuminé. Les chaussures semblent ainsi en suspension dans l'espace lorsqu'elles sont éclairées par des spots. Mais c'est l'intérieur de cet immeuble du XIXe siècle qui réserve le plus de surprises architecturales. Un plastique polyacrylique translucide moulé sous vide constitue le plafond et les présentoirs intégrés. Le sol est recouvert de verre serti dans d'autres panneaux en acrylique. Les sièges, la caisse et les vitrines d'accessoires blanc brillant s'inspirent d'un « style Barbarella et de formes ovoïdes » selon les architectes. Mais c'est encore l'éclairage qui est le plus surprenant. 540 ampoules fluorescentes programmées par ordinateur sont disposées derrière la coque de plastique, ce qui permet de moduler l'ambiance lumineuse selon une gamme de couleurs choisies. Une seconde boutique Shoebaloo a été conçue par les architectes pour Rotterdam. En évoquant Barbarella, Meyer en Van Schooten désignent une période récente de l'histoire du design qui les intéresse, même s'ils ont interprété ce thème à travers un goût et des technologies résolument contemporains.

The futuristic interior of the shop has a continuous design that allows the products displayed to be viewed without distraction, despite the strong architectural presence.

Trotz der starken architektonischen Präsenz lenkt das futuristische Innere des Ladens dank durchgängiger Gestaltung nicht von der Präsentation der Produkte ab.

L'intérieur futuriste du magasin suit un plan continu qui permet de regarder les produits sans être distrait par la forte présence de l'architecture.

A chart (below) shows the preprogrammed color variations that have been arranged for the fluorescent lighting system. The images above and to the right show two variations on the color scheme.

Die Grafik (unten) zeigt die einprogrammierten Farbwechsel der fluoreszierenden Beleuchtung. Die Bilder oben und rechts demonstrieren zwei verschiedene Farbschemata.

Un diagramme (ci-dessous) montre la programmation des variations de couleur prévues pour le système d'éclairage fluorescent. Ci-dessus et à droite : deux variantes de la programmation chromatique.

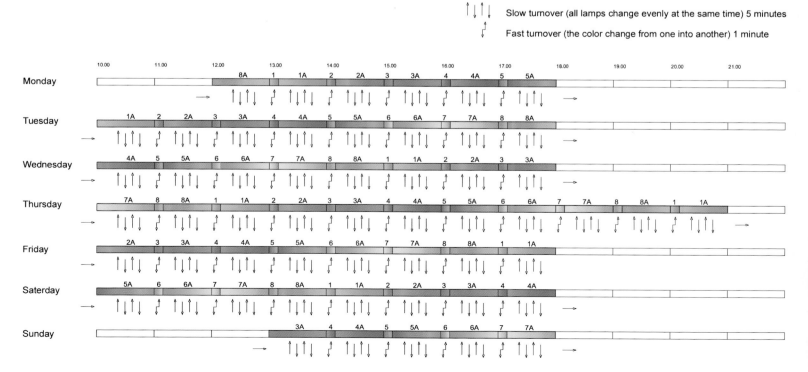

BLOK 3
ALMERE
2002 - 07

FLOOR AREA: Public Library, 11 000 m²; Shops, 2200 m²;
Spare capacity for library 3000 m², plus 30 apartments
CLIENT: City of Almere,
Dienst Stadcentrum and Almere Hart CV
COST: €23 million

Created on land reclaimed from the sea in the province of Flevoland in 1977, Almere grew rapidly without having any historic center. The 2005 population of 175 000 is expected to surge to 215 000 by 2010. Asked in 1994 to create a master plan for a new center, Rem Koolhaas and OMA proposed in 1997 to divide the area into districts, each with its own character. The heart of the city is divided into two levels intended to separate shoppers from other traffic, undoubtedly proving Koolhaas's theory that shopping is the driving force behind architecture in general. Architects such as Alsop & Störmer, Claus en Kaan, and Kazuyo Sejima (SANAA) have participated in the project. Blok 3, which is under the responsibility of Meyer en Van Schooten contains an 11 000 m² public library, 2200 m² of shop space, 3000 m² of spare space for the library, and 30 owner-occupied apartments. Blok 3 has a triangular plan and is divided into two sections—a four-story base containing shops, and the library with its spare space—and a rectangular five-story block of apartments in the southeast corner of the site. Surrounded by glass-façade buildings, Blok 3 was made intentionally "robust" by the architects, rising "from the ground like a massive cliff." Coarse-grained concrete panels with fragments of stone and glass set in them emphasize the contrast with neighboring buildings. The architects are designing the office and service areas, while the library interior is being created in collaboration with the Amsterdam firm Concrete Architectural Associates.

Die Stadt Almere entstand ab 1977 in der dem Meer abgerungenen Neulandprovinz Flevoland und wuchs schnell, hatte aber kein Zentrum. Es wird erwartet, dass die Einwohnerzahl bis 2010 von 175 000 (2005) auf 215 000 ansteigen wird. Rem Koolhaas und OMA wurden 1994 mit dem Entwurf des Masterplans für eine neue Stadtmitte beauftragt und schlugen 1997 vor, das Gebiet in Viertel aufzuteilen, jedes mit einem eigenen Charakter. Die Stadtmitte ist in zwei Ebenen unterteilt, um Fußgänger- und anderen Verkehr in den Einkaufsbereichen zu trennen. Dies entspricht Koolhaas' Theorie vom Konsum als Antriebskraft der Architektur. Architekten wie Alsop & Störmer, Claus en Kaan und Kazuyo Sejima (SANAA) haben an diesem Projekt mitgewirkt. Blok 3 von Meyer en Van Schooten umfasst eine öffentliche Bücherei (11 000 m²), die später auch erweitert werden kann, Ladenflächen (2200 m²) und 30 Eigentumswohnungen. Blok 3 hat einen dreieckigen

Grundriss und ist in zwei Abschnitte unterteilt – eine viergeschossige Basis mit Geschäften und der Bibliothek mit vorgesehener Erweiterung und den rechteckigen, fünfgeschossigen Wohnblock in der südöstlichen Ecke des Baugeländes. Umgeben von Gebäuden mit Glasfassaden wurde Blok 3 von den Architekten absichtlich „robust" gestaltet und sollte „aus dem Erdboden wie eine massive Klippe aufragen". Grobkörnige Betonplatten mit eingegossenen Stein- und Glasfragmenten betonen den Kontrast zu den benachbarten Gebäuden. Die Architekten zeichnen auch verantwortlich für die Gestaltung der Büros und Nebenräume, während die Innenausstattung der Bibliothek in Zusammenarbeit mit dem Amsterdamer Büro Concrete Architectural Associates entsteht.

Construite sur des terres récupérées sur la mer dans la province du Flevoland en 1977, la ville d'Almere a connu une croissance rapide sans posséder pour autant de centre historique. Sa population de 175 000 habitants en 2005 devrait en compter 215 000 en 2010. Chargés en 1994 du plan directeur du nouveau centre, Rem Koolhaas et OMA ont proposé en 1997 de répartir la zone en quartiers, chacun doté de son propre caractère. Le cœur de la cité est divisé en deux niveaux pour séparer les piétons des autres circulations, illustrant la théorie de Koolhaas pour lequel le commerce est la force motrice de l'architecture en général. Des architectes comme Alsop & Störmer, Claus en Kaan et Kazuyo Sejima (SANAA) ont participé au projet. Le Blok 3, sous la responsabilité de Meyer en Van Schooten contient une bibliothèque publique de 11 000 m² et ses 3000 m² de réserves, 2200 m² d'espaces commerciaux et 30 appartements en copropriété. Le plan d'ensemble triangulaire est divisé en deux sections : une base sur quatre niveaux contenant les magasins et l'ensemble de la bibliothèque – et un bloc rectangulaire d'appartements de cinq niveaux à l'angle sud-est du terrain. Habillé de façades de verre, le Blok 3 se veut « robuste s'élevant du sol à la manière d'une falaise ». Des panneaux de béton à surface brute incrustée de fragments de pierre et de verre accentuent le contraste avec les immeubles voisins. Les architectes ont conçu les bureaux et les zones de services tandis que l'intérieur de la bibliothèque a été aménagé en collaboration avec l'agence amstellodamoise Concrete Architectural Associates.

With its cantilevered and raised forward surface, Blok 3 has some relation to the firm's earlier ING Group Headquarters building in Amsterdam. A layered or sedimentary appearance emphasizes the continuity and dynamic aspect of the large structure.

Mit seiner vorkragenden und aufgeständerten Front hat Blok 3 Ähnlichkeit mit dem Hauptsitz der ING Group in Amsterdam. Der Eindruck von Schichtung oder Sedimentablagerung betont den Zusammenhang der Gebäudeteile und steigert deren dynamische Wirkung.

Avec son porte-à-faux et sa projection vers l'avant, le Blok 3 n'est pas sans relation avec le siège du Groupe ING antérieurement réalisé par l'agence à Amsterdam. L'aspect stratifié ou sédimenté met en valeur la continuité et la dynamique de cette très vaste réalisation.

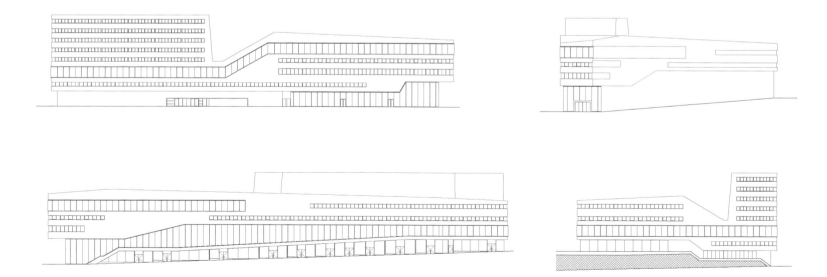

Despite its strong massing and considerable length, the architecture is both convivial and attractive. A marked contrast is offered between the rough cladding and the long, smooth glazed surface.

Trotz der Kompaktheit und beträchtlichen Länge des Gebäudes erscheint die Architektur freundlich und einladend. Das raue Mauerwerk und die langen, glatten verglasten Flächen bieten einen starken Kontrast.

Malgré des masses puissantes et une longueur considérable, l'immeuble est à la fois convivial et attirant. Un contraste marqué a été créé entre la texture rugueuse de l'habillage et les immenses plans vitrés.

MVRDV

MVRDV
Dunantstraat 10
3024 BC Rotterdam

Tel: +31 10 4 77 28 60
Fax: +31 10 4 77 36 27
e-mail: office@mvrdv.nl
Web: www.mvrdv.nl

MVRDV was created in 1991 by Winy Maas, Jacob van Rijs and Nathalie de Vries. The name of the firm is made up of the initials of the surnames of its partners. Born in 1959 in Schijndel, Maas, like his two partners, studied at the Technical University in Delft. Jacob van Rijs was born in Amsterdam in 1964, and Nathalie de Vries in Appingedam in 1964. Both Maas and Van Rijs worked for OMA. Maas and De Vries worked in the office of Ben van Berkel before founding MVRDV, and Nathalie de Vries also worked with Mecanoo in Delft. Aside from the Villa VPRO, Hilversum (1997), their work includes the RVU Building in Hilversum (1994–97); the Double House in Utrecht (1995–97, together with de Architectengroep); as well as WoZoCo, 100 apartments for elderly people, Amsterdam-Osdorp (1997). The architects designed the spectacular Dutch Pavilion at Expo 2000 in Hanover. Their plan for a pavilion that would have completely engulfed the Serpentine Gallery in London was delayed for technical reasons in 2004. MVRDV have also worked on urban-development schemes, such as their "Shadow City Bergen Op Zoom" project (1993); the master plan for Parklane Airport, Eindhoven, and the master plan for Subdivision 10 in Ypenburg. They participated in the competition for Les Halles in Paris (2004) and have worked on plans for the possible Olympic Village in New York (2012).

LLOYD HOTEL
AMSTERDAM
1998 - 2004

FLOOR AREA: 8300 m²
CLIENT: Woonstichting de Key, Amsterdam
COST: €10.5 million

The Lloyd Hotel is located at the Oostelijke Handelskade near Amsterdam's Central Station. This two-kilometer-long island, mainly intended for warehouses, was created in 1875 when sailing ships were being replaced by larger steamboats. The "Koninklijke Hollandsche Lloyd" (KHL) shipping company had its headquarters here. During World War I, the firm asked the architect Evert Breman to design a hotel for emigrants on the island. The Lloyd Hotel opened in 1921 and was in use as such until 1935. Converted into a prison by the Germans, the building was used for that purpose until 1989, when the city of Amsterdam rented it to the Spinoza Foundation for use by artists. A decade later the building was abandoned which is when MVRDV were asked to renovate the structure and return it to its original use. Although they retained the historic brick façades, the architects completely rethought the 8300 m² interior, creating a three-story opening aligned with the main entrance, where a restaurant and bar are located. Stairways lead up from this space to the rooms and also to the Cultural Embassy, a library and an area intended to inform visitors on the lively arts scene of Amsterdam. Indeed art works and design characterize the interiors and give the rather gray exterior of the hotel an inner luminosity and modernity. Although it still has rather desolate stretches, the Oostelijke Handelskade has become quite fashionable and the Lloyd Hotel is in the midst of an ambitious construction zone that includes offices, housing, and such night spots as the neighboring Panama Club.

Das Lloyd Hotel in der Nähe des Hauptbahnhofs von Amsterdam steht an der Oostelijke Handelskade. Dieser Kai ist eigentlich eine mit Hafenspeichern bebaute, 2 km lange künstliche Insel, die 1875 angelegt wurde, als größere Dampfschiffe die alten Segelschiffe verdrängten. Die Reederei Koninklijke Hollandsche Lloyd (KHL) hatte dort ihren Hauptsitz. Gegen Ende des Ersten Weltkriegs beauftragte die KHL den Architekten Evert Breman mit dem Bau eines Hotels für Emigranten auf der Insel. Das Lloyd Hotel wurde 1921 eröffnet und bis 1935 betrieben. Die Deutschen bauten es zum Gefängnis um, und als solches wurde das Gebäude genutzt, bis die Stadt Amsterdam es 1989 der Spinoza-Stiftung zur Nutzung durch Künstler vermietete. Ein Jahrzehnt später stand es leer, als MVRDV den Auftrag erhielten, es zu sanieren und der ursprünglichen Nutzung wieder zuzuführen. Die Architekten restaurierten die historischen Fassaden, strukturierten die nicht denk-malgeschützten Bereiche im Inneren (8300 m² Geschossfläche) jedoch völlig um. Hinter dem Haupteingang schufen sie einen dreigeschossigen Luftraum, in dem sie ein Restaurant und eine Bar unterbrachten. Treppen führen von dieser Halle zu den Zimmern, zur Bibliothek und „Kulturbotschaft", d. h. einem Bereich, in dem sich die Hotelgäste über das lebendige Kunst- und Kulturleben in der Stadt informieren können. Kunst und Design beleben auch die Räume des Hotels und verleihen ihnen im Kontrast zum grauen Äußeren des Gebäudes Leuchtkraft und Modernität. Obwohl die Oostelijke Handelskade stellenweise noch etwas trostlos wirkt, liegt die Gegend im Trend. Das Lloyd Hotel steht mitten in einem ambitionierten Neubauviertel mit Büros, Wohnungen und nächtlichen Attraktionen wie dem benachbarten Panama Club.

Le Lloyd Hotel se trouve à Oostelijke Handelskade près de la gare centrale d'Amsterdam. Cette île de deux kilomètres de long fut créée en 1875 pour accueillir des entrepôts au moment du passage de la marine à voile aux bateaux à vapeur. La société de transports maritimes KHL (Koninklijke Hollandsche Lloyd) y avait son siège. Pendant la Première Guerre mondiale, la KHL demanda à l'architecte Evert Breman de construire un hôtel pour émigrés qui ouvrit en 1921 et fut utilisé jusqu'en 1935. Transformé en prison par les Allemands pendant la Seconde Guerre, il conserva cette fonction jusqu'en 1989, date à laquelle la ville d'Amsterdam le loua à la Fondation Spinoza pour les artistes. Dix années plus tard, le bâtiment fut abandonné et l'on demanda à MVRDV de rénover l'ensemble et de le rendre à sa destination première. Tout en conservant les façades de brique historiques, les architectes ont entièrement repensé les 8300 m² de l'intérieur et créé un atrium sur trois niveaux dans l'axe de l'entrée principale, où sont venus se loger un bar et un restaurant. Des escaliers conduisent aux chambres et à l'Ambassade culturelle, bibliothèque et zone d'information sur les arts vivants à Amsterdam. Les œuvres d'art et le design confèrent une grande originalité aux aménagements intérieurs modernes et lumineux en dépit d'une apparence extérieure assez terne. Bien qu'encore en partie assez vide, l'Oostelijke Handelskade devient à la mode et le Lloyd Hotel se retrouve au milieu d'une ambitieuse zone de bureaux, de logements et d'établissements nocturnes dont le tout proche Panama Club.

Mezzanine areas above the main dining space offer a selection of publications and lend form to the client's idea of a "cultural embassy."

Über dem Hauptspeisesaal liegen mehrere Zwischenebenen mit Lesezonen. Sie verkörpern das, was die Auftraggeber als „Kulturbotschaft" bezeichnen.

Les mezzanines au-dessus de la salle à manger principale offrent une sélection de publications et incarnent le souhait du client de créer une « ambassade culturelle ».

To the right, the dining room. Below, a
stairway and hall in the hotel and, to the
right below, the almost unaltered original
façade of the building.

Rechts Blick in den Speisesaal.
Unten Treppe und Korridor im Hotel, rechts
unten die fast vollständig original belassene
Fassade des Altbaus.

À droite, la salle à manger. Ci-dessous, un
escalier et un hall, en bas à droite, la façade
originale laissée pratiquement intacte.

Guest rooms and common spaces in the hotel retain much of the port flavor of the original building and its frequently nautical décor.

In Gästezimmern und Gemeinschaftsräumen des Hotels blieb viel von der Atmosphäre und vom nautischen Dekor des alten Hafengebäudes bewahrt.

Les chambres et les espaces communs conservent beaucoup de l'atmosphère de port du bâtiment d'origine et de son décor d'inspiration fréquemment nautique.

The architects bring a moderated modernity to the Lloyd Hotel, making use where possible of existing configurations and décor, and elsewhere, adding what is necessary to make the building function as a hotel.

Die Architekten haben das Lloyd Hotel zurückhaltend modern ausgestattet, wobei sie soweit möglich die vorhandenen Räumlichkeiten und Dekore beibehielten und hinzufügten, was für den modernen Hotel-betrieb des Gebäudes notwendig war.

Les architectes ont insufflé à cet ancien bâtiment une modernité modérée en conservant à chaque fois que c'était possible la configuration et le décor existants, ajoutant ce qui lui était nécessaire pour remplir sa nouvelle fonction hôtelière.

Where facilities like bathrooms were missing in the original building, MVRDV adds them with a practical sense of volumes and function. Bathroom furnishings are by Bureau Lakenvelder/MVRDV and Joep van Lieshout.

Wo moderner Komfort fehlte, wurde er mit viel Sinn für Raumgefühl und praktischen Nutzen ergänzt. Die Badezimmer wurden vom Büro Lakenvelder/MVRDV und Joep van Lieshout entworfen.

Lorsque certains équipements manquaient, comme les salles de bains, MVRDV les a ajoutés dans un esprit très pratique d'intégration des fonctions et des volumes. L'aménagement des salles de bains a été conçu par le Bureau Lakenvelder/MVRDV et Joep van Lieshout.

In part because it was not designed as a hotel, the building offers a variety of spaces and types of rooms that would not be found in a purpose-built structure. In some rooms rather daring contemporary solutions are used to make existing space function as a hotel suite (right).

Da das Gebäude ursprünglich nicht als Hotel gebaut wurde, bietet es eine Reihe von Räumen und Raumtypen, die in Hotel-neubauten fehlen. Für einige Bereiche erfand man kühne zeitgenössische Lösungen, um die Räume als Hotelsuiten nutzbar zu machen (rechts).

En partie parce qu'il n'a pas été conçu pour être un hôtel, le bâtiment offre une grande variété d'espaces et de types de chambres que l'on ne trouverait pas dans une construction fonctionnelle. Dans certaines chambres assez audacieuses, des solutions contemporaines ont été choisies pour que le volume existant se transforme réellement en suite d'hôtel (à droite).

PATIO HOUSING
YPENBURG
1999 - 2002

FLOOR AREA: 110 to 180 m²
CLIENT: Amvest
COST: €7 million

In order to deal with the population density and rising demand for housing, the Dutch government devised the so-called VINEX plan in the early 1990s. The goal was to create 750 000 housing units or apartments between 1995 and 2015, along lines partially inspired by American suburban housing developments. Further, these new residences were to be situated in new "compact cities" located near existing urban centers and well connected to their transportation infrastructure. One of these new areas, located between The Hague, Delft and Rotterdam, is Ypenburg. A master plan for the town was laid out by Frits Palmboom, calling for 12 000 dwellings to be built on the site of a former airport. Five "theme districts" intended to have different atmospheres were called for. One area, called Subdivision 10, with a quota of 768 units, came under the supervision of MVRDV, who created their own master plan, in collaboration with the developer Amvest, and contributed two groups of residences, respectively, called the Patio Houses and Hageneiland Housing. Near other housing designed by Herman Hertzberger, Claus en Kaan and John Bosch, the work of MVRDV has been extensively praised for breaking up the monotony typical of such housing developments. In December 2002, Aaron Betsky, Director of the Netherlands Architecture Institute, gave MVRDV's Hageneiland housing the NAI Prize as the best project that year by Dutch architects under the age of 40. He declared that their work was "remarkable even by Dutch standards." The jury called the design "a very elegant reaction against uniformity." Working with very tight budgetary constraints, the architects have been criticized for giving more importance to appearance than to interiors. "We did make a decision early on to concentrate on the idea of exterior atmosphere," comments Jacob van Rijs from MVRDV. "The cost of that," he concludes "was that we didn't have as much to spend on the interiors."

Anfang der 1990er Jahre lancierte die niederländische Regierung angesichts der wachsenden Bevölkerungsdichte das VINEX-Programm zur Deckung des dringenden Bedarfs an Wohnraum. Es sah vor, von 1995 bis 2015, teils nach dem Vorbild amerikanischer vorstädtischer Wohnungsbauprogramme, 750 000 Wohneinheiten zu schaffen, und zwar in „neuen kompakten Städten" mit optimalen Nahverkehrsanbindungen zu bestehenden Städten. Eine dieser neuen Städte ist Ypenburg im Gebiet zwischen Den Haag, Delft und Rotterdam. Frits Palmboom erstellte den Masterplan, der 12 000 Wohnungen auf dem Gelände eines ehemaligen Flughafens vorsah, verteilt über fünf „Themenbezirke" mit jeweils eigenem Charakter. Mit der Planung des Teilgebiet 10 genannten Viertels (768 Wohnungen) wurden MVRDV beauftragt. Zusammen mit der Bauträgerfirma Amvest entwarfen sie den Masterplan und zwei Gruppen von Wohngebäuden, die Patio-Häuser und die Siedlung Hageneiland. Das Projekt von MVRDV, in dessen Nähe auch Bauten

von Herman Hertzberger, Claus en Kaan und John Bosch stehen, wurde weithin dafür gelobt, dass es die typische Monotonie solcher Wohnbebauungen vermeidet. Im Dezember 2002 zeichnete Aaron Betsky, Direktor des Niederländischen Architekturinstituts, die Hageneiland-Bebauung von MVRDV mit dem NAI-Preis für den besten Entwurf des Jahres von Architekten unter 40 aus und erklärte, ihre Arbeiten seien „selbst an niederländischen Standards gemessen bemerkenswert". Die Jury bezeichnete das Projekt als „eine höchst elegante Reaktion auf Uniformität". Den Architekten stand nur ein äußerst knapp bemessenes Budget zur Verfügung und sie sind dafür kritisiert worden, dass sie dem äußeren Erscheinungsbild mehr Aufmerksamkeit schenkten als etwa den Interieurs. „Bereits in einem frühen Stadium beschlossen wir tatsächlich, uns auf die äußere Atmosphäre zu konzentrieren", erklärt Jacob van Rijs. „Die Folge war natürlich, dass uns für die Innenräume nicht mehr so viel Geld zur Verfügung stand."

C'est pour répondre à la densité de la population et une demande croissante de logements que le gouvernement néerlandais a proposé le plan Vinex au début des années 1990. L'objectif était de créer 750 000 maisons ou appartements de 1995 à 2015, selon une approche inspirée de l'urbanisme des banlieues américaines. Par ailleurs, ces nouvelles résidences devaient être situées dans de nouvelles « villes compactes » situées à proximité des centres urbains et bien reliées aux infrastructures de transports. Ypenburg est l'une de ces zones nouvelles, entre La Haye, Rotterdam et Delft. Le plan directeur établi par Frits Palmboom prévoyait 12 000 logements sur le site d'un ancien aéroport. Cinq « districts à thème » présentant des atmosphères différentes furent mis en place. La Subdivision 10, une zone de 768 logements, fut confiée à MVRDV qui mit au point son propre plan d'urbanisme, en collaboration avec le promoteur Amvest, intégrant deux groupes de résidences les Patio Houses et Hageneiland Housing. Voisine d'autres logements conçus par Herman Hertzberger, Claus en Kaan ou John Bosch, cette réalisation a été applaudie pour avoir su rompre avec la monotonie caractéristique de ce type de projet en général. En décembre 2002, Aaron Betsky, qui dirigeait à l'époque l'Institut de l'Architecture Néerlandaise, remit à ce projet le prix NAI de meilleur projet de l'année par de jeunes architectes nationaux de moins de quarante ans. Il déclara que leur œuvre était « remarquable, y compris selon les critères néerlandais ». Le jury qualifia le projet de « très élégante réaction contre l'uniformité ». Travaillant sous de fortes contraintes budgétaires, les architectes ont été critiqués pour avoir donné plus d'importance à l'aspect extérieur qu'à l'intérieur ... « Nous avons pris la décision très tôt de nous concentrer sur l'atmosphère extérieure », a commenté Jacob van Rijs, « le coût de cette option est que nous ne disposons pas d'autant de moyens à consacrer à l'intérieur. »

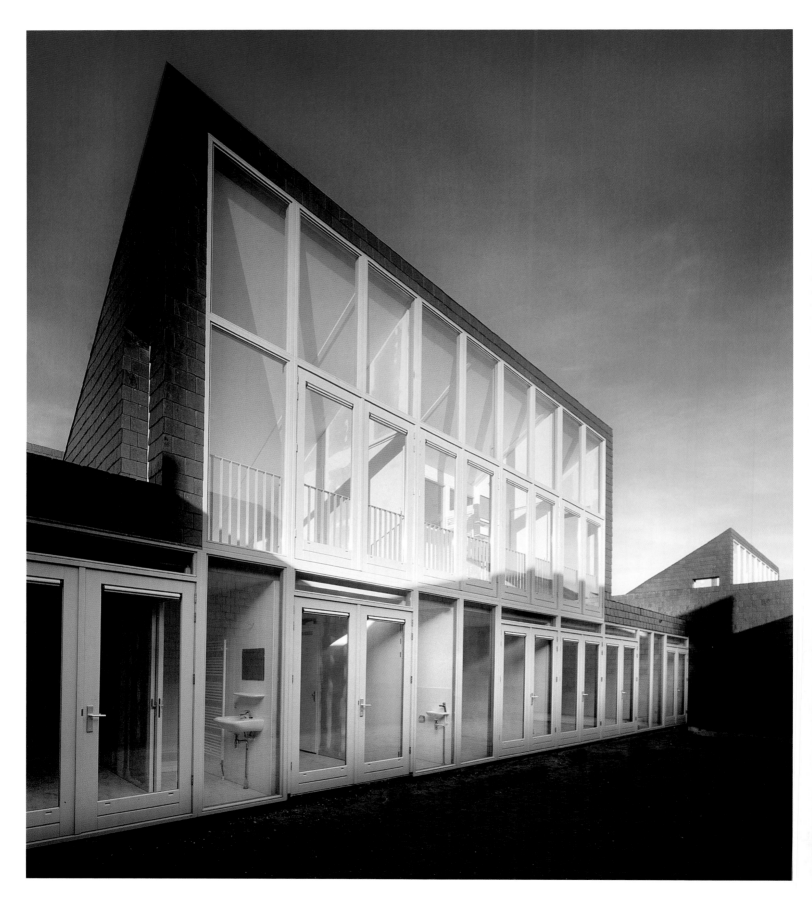

Though public housing is always a difficult exercise in budget balancing, the architects have taken to the task with typical Dutch pragmatism.

Obwohl öffentlicher Wohnungsbau immer das Jonglieren mit knappen Budgets bedeutet, nahmen die Architekten sich der Aufgabe mit typisch niederländischem Pragmatismus an.

Bien que le logement social soit toujours un exercice budgétaire délicat, les architectes se sont plongés dans cette tâche avec un pragmatisme tout néerlandais.

An austere, repetitive design brings to mind a long tradition of modestly scaled row houses often seen in the Netherlands.

Die konsequent serielle Gestaltung stellt die Häuser in die Tradition der in den Niederlanden weit verbreiteten einfachen Reihenhäuser.

Le plan répétitif et austère rappelle une longue tradition d'alignements de maisons modestes que l'on voit souvent aux Pays-Bas.

6

NEUTELINGS RIEDIJK

**NEUTELINGS RIEDIJK
ARCHITECTEN BV**
Stationsplein 45 unit A5.004
3013 AK Rotterdam

Tel: +31 10 4 04 66 77
Fax: +31 10 4 14 27 12
e-mail: info@neutelings-riedijk.com
Web: www.neutelings-riedijk.com

WILLEM JAN NEUTELINGS was born in 1959 in Bergen-op-Zoom. He studied at the Technical University in Delft before working for OMA with Rem Koolhaas (1977–86). He has taught at the Academy of Architecture in Rotterdam and at the Berlage Institute in Amsterdam (1990–99). MICHIEL RIEDIJK was born in Geldrop in 1964. He attended the Technical University in Delft (1983–89) before working with J. D. Bekkering in Amsterdam. He has taught at the Technical University in Delft and Eindhoven and at the Academies of Architecture in Amsterdam, Rotterdam and Maastricht. Their built work includes the Prinsenhoek Residential Complex, Sittard (1992–95); Tilburg Housing (1993–96); Hollainhof Social Housing, Ghent, Belgium (1993–98); Borneo Sporenburg Housing, Amsterdam (1994–97); Lakeshore Housing, First phase, Huizen (1994–96); and the Building for Veenman Printers, Ede (1995–97). One of their most widely publicized projects was the Minnaert Building, Utrecht (1994–98). They have also built fire stations in Breda (1996–98) and Maastricht (1996–99). In 2004, they won the competition for the Kolizej Centre in Ljubljana, Slovenia, which is to include a 1400-seat concert hall, 25 000 m² of office space, 100 apartments, a shopping arcade, and a parking lot.

5 SFINXEN HOUSING

HUIZEN 2000 - 03

SIZE: 70 apartments
CLIENT: Bouwfonds Wonen Noord-West
COST: €11 million

This unexpected project was the result of a 1994 competition. A total of 70 apartments are located in five buildings on the Gooimeerpromenade in Huizen. Each of the nearly identical blocks tapers toward the water to offer the best possible unobstructed lake views. Each floor of the buildings contains one less apartment, resulting in a configuration that the architects have likened to the form of the sphinx. The sun-oriented "back" of each sphinx is used for the apartments' terraces. The penthouse in each building is slightly different, "giving rise to a rhythm of distinctive heads, a striking skyline seen from the shore approach of the Stichtse bridge linking the new polders and the old mainland." The buildings are clad in aluminum and have parking facilities located below the water level. Reeds are planted along the sides of the concrete landing platforms that link the buildings to their entrances. An emphasis has also been placed on public spaces along an esplanade between the buildings that successively gives way to a "look-out bastion, a surf beach, a village square, a wind balcony and a fishing jetty," as described by the architects. An image of this complex figures on the cover of the 2003–04 NAI Yearbook *Architecture in the Netherlands*, a confirmation that the design has captured the imagination of the architectural community.

Diese originelle Anlage – insgesamt 70 Wohnungen in fünf Gebäuden an der Gooimeerpromenade in Huizen – ist das Ergebnis eines Architekturwettbewerbs von 1994. Die fast identischen Wohnblöcke verjüngen sich zur offenen Wasserfläche hin und bieten so den Bewohnern bestmögliche Ausblicke auf den See. Von Stockwerk zu Stockwerk befindet sich eine Wohnung weniger. Das ergab eine Bauform, die von den Architekten mit einer Sphinx verglichen wurde. Balkonterrassen auf der Sonnenseite bilden den „Rücken" jeder Sphinx. Die fünf Penthäuser sind unterschiedlich gestaltet, was „einen Rhythmus charakteristischer Köpfe ergibt, von der Stichtse-Brücke zwischen den neuen Polderlandschaft und dem alten Festland aus gesehen eine auffällige Silhouette". Die Bauten sind mit Aluminium verkleidet und und haben Tiefgaragen unterhalb des Seespiegels. Beiderseits der Betonpiers, die von den Tiefgaragen zu den Haupteingängen führen, wurde Schilf angepflanzt. Großen Wert legten die Architekten auf die Gestaltung der öffentlichen Flächen entlang der Uferpromenade, „die zu einer Ausguckbastion führt, einem Strand für Surfer, einem Dorfplatz, einem ‚Windbalkon' und einer Mole für Angler", so die Architekten. Eine Abbildung dieser Anlage ziert die Umschlagseite des NAI Jahrbuchs *Architektur in den Niederlanden* 2003-04 und beweist, dass dieser Entwurf unter Architekten großen Anklang gefunden hat.

Ce curieux projet est issu d'un concours organisé en 1994. Il regroupe soixante-dix appartements réunis dans cinq immeubles édifiés sur la Gooimeerpromenade à Huizen. Chaque construction, presque identique, s'incline vers l'eau pour offrir la meilleure vue possible sur le lac. Le nombre d'appartements par niveau décroît peu à peu pour dessiner une configuration que les architectes ont comparée à la forme d'un sphinx. Le « dos » de chaque sphinx, orienté vers le soleil, est utilisé pour les terrasses des logements. La penthouse est légèrement différente dans chaque immeuble « ce qui génère un rythme de ‹têtes› différentes qui forme un panorama surprenant vu du pont de Stichtse, lequel réunit les nouveaux polders à la terre ferme ». Les immeubles sont habillés d'aluminium et possèdent des parkings en dessous du niveau de l'eau. Des joncs sont plantés le long des passerelles de béton qui relient l'immeuble au sol. L'accent a également été placé sur les espaces publics le long de l'esplanade entre les immeubles qui laisse place successivement à un « bastion d'observation, une plage de surf, une place de village, un ‹balcon des vents› et une jetée des pêcheurs », selon le descriptif des architectes. Ce projet a su capter l'attention de la communauté architecturale et figure en couverture de l'ouvrage annuel de la NAI, *Architecture in the Netherlands* 2003-04.

Like ships pulled into dock but looking out to sea, the Sfinxen Housing calls on various aspects of Dutch tradition in its configuration and location.

Wie Schiffe im Hafendock – aber mit dem Bug zur See – greifen die Sfinxen-Wohnblöcke, was ihre Platzierung und formale Gestaltung angeht, verschiedene Aspekte der niederländischen Bautradition auf.

Comme des bateaux ancrés dans le port mais regardant vers la mer, les maisons Sfinxen évoquent de nombreux aspects de tradition néerlandaise dans leur configuration et leur implantation.

SHIPPING AND TRANSPORT COLLEGE
ROTTERDAM
2000 - 05

FLOOR AREA: 30 000 m^2
CLIENT: Stichting Scheepvaart en
Transportonderwijs Rotterdam, Erik Hietbrink
COST: €42 million

Located on the Lloyd Pier in Rotterdam, a former harbor area that overlooks the Maas River, the new headquarters of the Shipping and Transport College is a singular, almost anthropomorphic presence. As the architects explain, "The idea of the building is to make a robust volume as an emblematic icon for the institute, referring to the sculptural harbor architecture of silos, cranes and ships rather than to the typical school or office building. Therefore, the complex has a strong sculptural zigzag shape, a kinked volume with a broad foot planted firmly on the quayside. The volume tapers upward to present a 70-meter-tall backward-leaning tower. At the top it widens again into a broad crown cantilevering 20 meters. Whereas the foot contains a large window directed towards the river, the head literally nods in the direction of the North Sea, like a giant periscope." The "head" of the tower contains a congress hall for 300 persons in the cantilevered volume, affording a spectacular view of the port and the North Sea. The 30 000 m^2 structure includes educational facilities, offices, a workshop and parking areas for the only independent vocational school for shipping, transport and logistics in the Netherlands recognized by the Dutch Ministry for Education, Culture and Science. The budget for the construction was €42 million. The architects were inspired by the maritime environment of the College, in particular by the walls of stacked shipping containers seen in the port of Rotterdam. They used a silver-gray and steel-blue checkerboard pattern of corrugated metal cladding on the façades, roofs and overhangs, forming "an unbroken industrial skin over the sculpture to further emphasize the maritime character of this starkly impressive building."

Auf dem Lloyd Pier von Rotterdam, im ehemaligen Hafengebiet an der Maas, steht der Neubau der Hochschule für Schifffahrts- und Transportwesen mit seiner einzigartigen, fast anthropomorphen Baugestalt. Ihre Absicht war, so die Architekten, anstelle des typischen Schul- oder Bürogebäudes „einen robusten Bau als prägnantes Symbol der Institution zu schaffen, mit Bezügen zur skulpturalen Hafenarchitektur mit Silos, Kränen und Schiffen". Deshalb entwarfen sie eine markante Zickzackform, einen abgeknickten Baukörper mit einem breiten Fuß fest auf dem Boden des Kais. Der Baukörper verjüngt sich nach oben und streckt sich in einen 70 m hohen, nach hinten geneigten Turm, der sich an der Spitze wiederum zu einer 20 m auskragenden Krone erweitert. Während der „Fuß" sich mit einem großen Fenster zum Fluss öffnet, neigt sich der „Kopf" wie ein riesiges Periskop zur Nordsee. Im auskragenden Teil beherbergt der „Kopf" eine Tagungshalle für 300

Personen, die einen fantastischen Blick über Hafen und Meer bietet. Das insgesamt 30 000 m^2 große Gebäude umfasst Hörsäle und Seminarräume, Büros, eine Werkstatt und Parkplätze der einzigen vom Ministerium für Erziehung, Kultur und Wissenschaft anerkannten Privatschule für Schifffahrts- und Transportwesen der Niederlande. Die Baukosten wurden auf 42 Millionen Euro veranschlagt. Die Architekten ließen sich von der maritimen Umgebung und den Schiffscontainern im Rotterdamer Hafen anregen und gestalteten Fassadenflächen, Dächer und Dachüberstände als Wellblechschachbrett in Silbergrau und Stahlblau. So erhielt „die Bauskulptur eine industrielle Haut, die den maritimen Charakter dieses eindrucksvollen Gebäudes hervorhebt".

C'est sur le Lloyd Pier à Rotterdam, ancienne zone portuaire en bordure de la Meuse, que le nouveau siège du Collège du transport maritime impose sa présence singulière, presque anthropomorphique. Comme l'explique son architecte : « L'idée de cet immeuble est de faire de ce robuste volume l'emblème de l'Institut, en se référant à l'architecture portuaire sculpturale des silos, des grues et des bateaux, plutôt qu'aux bâtiments classiques d'écoles ou de bureaux. C'est pourquoi il présente cette forme sculpturale en zigzag, celle d'un volume vrillé qui s'appuie cependant fermement sur le quai. Il se rétrécit vers le haut en une tour de 70 m de haut inclinée vers l'arrière. Au sommet, il retrouve sa largeur dans une important couronnement en porte-à-faux de 20 m. Alors que la base contient une immense baie ouverte sur le fleuve, le haut regarde vers la mer du Nord, à la manière d'un périscope géant. » La « tête » de la tour contient une salle de congrès de 300 places dans le volume en porte-à-faux et offre une vue spectaculaire sur le port et la mer. Les 30 000 m^2 de l'ensemble réunissent des installations d'enseignement, des bureaux, un atelier et des parkings nécessaires à la seule école professionnelle indépendante pour le transport maritime des Pays-Bas reconnue par le Ministère de l'éducation, de la culture et de la science. Le budget de construction est de 42 millions d'euros. Empruntant leurs sources à l'environnement maritime du collège, les architectes se sont inspirés des murs de conteneurs empilés que l'on aperçoit dans le port de Rotterdam. Comme ils l'expliquent, ils ont utilisé un habillage métallique en damier gris-argent et bleu acier pour les façades, les toitures et les porte-à-faux, qui forme « une peau industrielle ininterrompue tendue sur la forme sculptée pour mettre encore davantage en valeur le caractère maritime de ce très impressionnant bâtiment ».

With its cyclopean-cantilevered overhang, the Shipping and Transport College defines an instantly recognizable profile on the edge of the port.

Mit ihrer „einäugigen" Auskragung ist die Hochschule für Schifffahrts- und Transport-wesen am Rand des Hafengebiets nicht zu übersehen.

Par son porte-à-faux cyclopéen, le Collège du transport maritime affirme un profil instantanément reconnaissable en bordure du port.

With cladding that might bring to mind rows of life vests, the auditorium continues the warm red glow seen around the escalator above.

Mit Wandverkleidungen, die an aufblasbare Schwimmwesten erinnern, setzt das Auditorium das warme Orangerot aus dem Bereich der Rolltreppen fort.

L'habillage de l'auditorium, qui rappelle à sa façon des empilements de gilets de sauvetage, reprend le rouge chaleureux aperçu dans l'escalier mécanique ci-dessus.

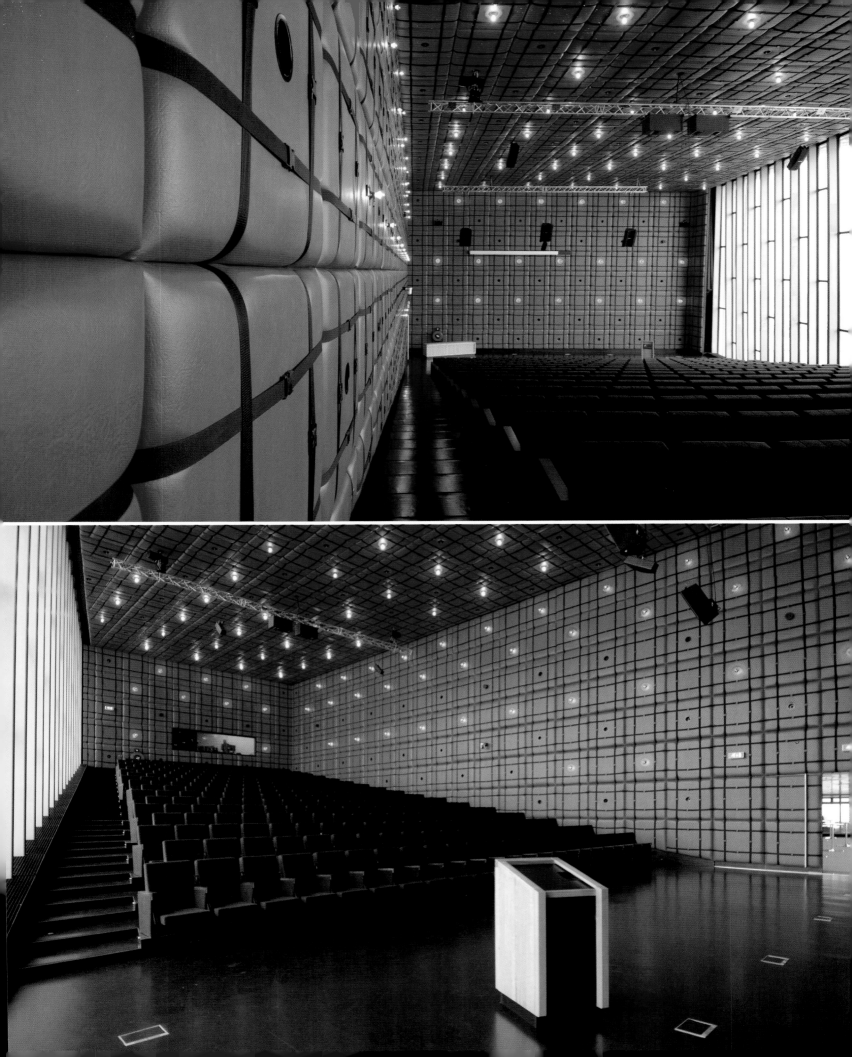

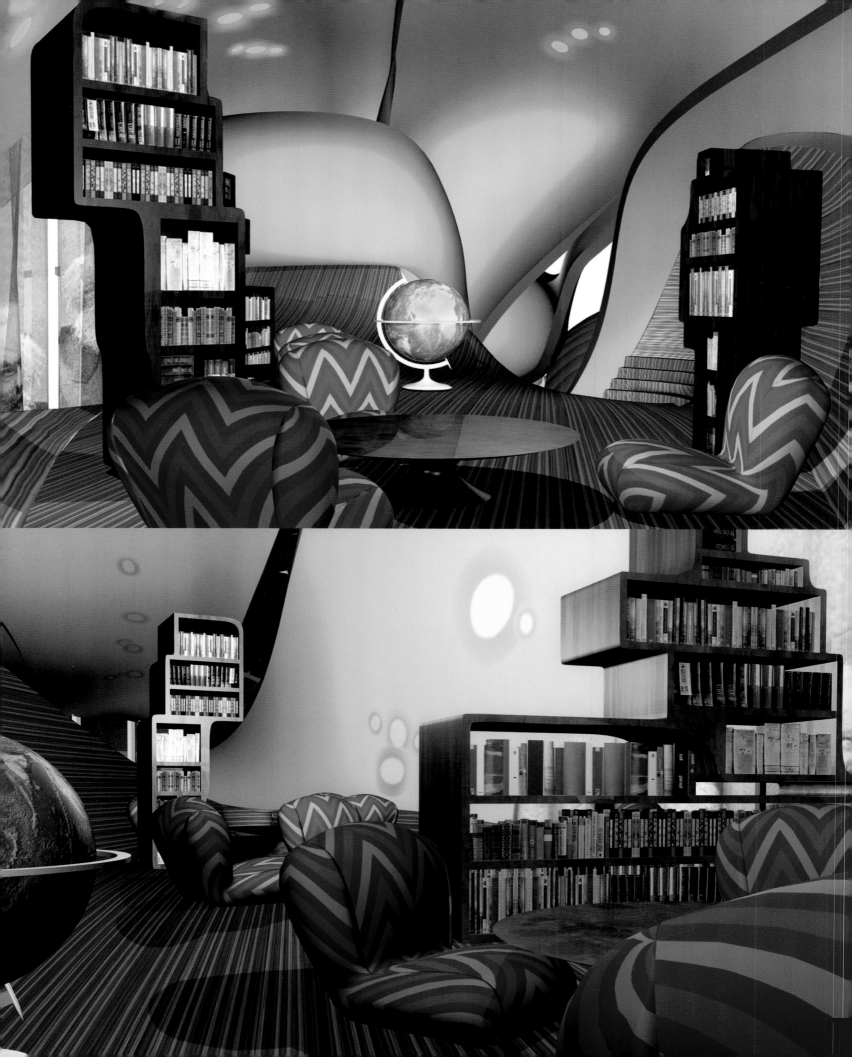

NOX

7

NOX/LARS SPUYBROEK
Heer Bokelweg 163
3032 AD Rotterdam

Tel/Fax: +31 10 4 77 28 53
e-mail: info@noxarch.com
Web: www.noxarch.com

LARS SPUYBROEK is the principal of NOX. Since the early 1990s, he has been involved in research on the relationship between architecture and media, often more specifically between architecture and computing. He was the editor-publisher of one of the first magazines on the subject (*NOX*, and later also *Forum*), has made videos (*Soft City*) and interactive electronic artworks (*Soft Site, edit Spline, deep Surface*). More recently, he has focused on architecture (H$_2$Oexpo, Blow Out, V2_lab, wetGRID, D-tower, Son-O-house, Maison Folie). His work has won several prizes and was shown at the Venice Biennale in 2000 and 2002. In 2003, NOX participated in the important international exhibitions "Zoomorphic" at the Victoria & Albert in London and "Non Standard Architecture" at the Centre Pompidou in Paris. NOX recently finished the interactive tower for the Dutch city of Doetinchem (D-Tower); "a house where sounds live" (Son-O-house); and a complex of cultural buildings in Lille, France (Maison Folie), as well as working on competitions for the European Central Bank in Frankfurt and the New Centre Pompidou in Metz, France (competition won by Shigeru Ban). Lars Spuybroek has lectured widely and has taught at several universities in Holland and is a regular visiting professor at Columbia University in New York. Since 2002, he has held a tenured professorship at the University of Kassel in Germany, where he chairs the CAD/digital design techniques department. His book, *Machining Architecture*, was published in 2004 (Thames & Hudson).

CLUB.HOUSE
ROTTERDAM
2004 -

FLOOR AREA: 860 m²
CLIENT: Rob Vester/Dura Vermeer
Development Rotterdam
COST: €1.8 million

This 860 m² clubhouse with library, restaurant, kitchen and guest rooms was designed by Lars Spuybroek with Hanna Stiller for a site located near Rotterdam Airport that "will function as a focal point in a community of luxury manors, as well as a regional high-quality restaurant and as a small life-style hotel for business people traveling between London and Rotterdam." Master planning for the park project was done by Ruurd Gietema, a partner of Kees Christiaanse (KCAP), and other participants in the architecture, aside from NOX and KCAP, are Zaha Hadid and Claus en Kaan. Working on the basis of "picturesque country house typologies," with a dome in the center and stretched gallery wings, Lars Spuybroek went on to imagine an entirely original configuration in which computer design plays an essential role. As he explains, "Structurally the Club.House is made of surfaces that cantilever from the middle zone, which functions as a large, porous, three-dimensional column, where the individual surfaces are made of a steel 'diagrid' structure of various densities, laser cut from steel plates. All panels consist of CNC-milled styrofoam (functioning both as mold and as insulation) covered with epoxy glass fiber laminate finished with a maroon-colored metallic coating. The panels are laid out in a herringbone pattern that, together with the extra ribbing of each panel and the overall double curvature of the structure, will give the Club.House an extremely sensuous appearance, making it unique in the Dutch (architectural) landscape."

Dieses Clubhaus mit Bibliothek, Restaurant, Küche und Gästezimmern auf insgesamt 860 m² entwarf Lars Spuybroek zusammen mit Hanna Stiller für ein Gebiet in der Nähe des Flughafens Rotterdam, das „einen Mittel- und Anziehungspunkt für die Bewohner der vielen umliegenden Herrenhäuser bilden und mit einem erstklassigen Restaurant und einem kleinen Lifestyle-Hotel auch für Geschäftsreisende zwischen London und Rotterdam attraktiv sein" soll. Ruurd Gietema, Partner von Kees Christiaanse (KCAP), zeichnete verantwortlich für den Masterplan; außer NOX und KCAP haben auch Zaha Hadid und Claus en Kaan Bauten für das Gebiet entworfen. Ausgehend vom „malerischen Landhaustyp" mit Kuppeldach in der Mitte und langgestreckten Seitenflügeln, schuf Lars Spuybroek eine höchst originelle Bauform, bei deren Entwicklung computergeneriertes Design die entscheidende Rolle spielte. „Die Konstruktion des Club.House besteht aus Flächen", so der Architekt, „die vom zentralen Bereich auskragen. Letzterer fungiert als große, poröse räumliche Säule, deren einzelne Oberflächen aus per Laser zugeschnittenen Stahlplatten bestehen und ein Konstruktionsraster von wechselnder Dichte bilden. Alle Paneele bestehen aus einem mit kastanienbraunem Metalliclack beschichteten, mit Epoxidharz verstärkten Glasfaserschichtstoff auf Styroporplatten, die mithilfe computernumerischer Steuerung geformt werden und als Gussform und Isolierung zugleich dienen. Die Paneele werden im Fischgrätmuster verlegt. Im Verbund mit der Stegverstärkung der Paneele und der Doppelkurvatur der Konstruktion wird das dem Club.House ein höchst sinnliches Aussehen geben und es zu einem ‚Unikat' in der niederländischen (Architektur-)Landschaft machen."

Ce club house de 860 m² comprenant une bibliothèque, un restaurant, une cuisine et des chambres a été conçu par Lars Spuybroek en collaboration avec Hanna Stiller pour un terrain voisin de l'aéroport de Rotterdam qui « sera le point d'attraction d'un ensemble comprenant des résidences de luxe, ainsi qu'un restaurant de qualité et un hôtel de charme pour hommes d'affaires voyageant entre Londres et Rotterdam ». Le plan directeur du projet de parc qui fait aussi appel à des architectes comme Zaha Hadid et Claus en Kaan est l'œuvre de Ruurd Gietema, associé de Kees Christiaanse (KCAP). Sur la base des « typologies de la maison de campagne pittoresque », grâce à une coupole centrale et des ailes-galeries, Spuybroek en est venu à imaginer une configuration entièrement originale dans laquelle la CAO a joué un rôle essentiel. Il explique que « structurellement, le Club.House est fait de surfaces en porte-à-faux par rapport à la zone centrale, qui fonctionne comme une énorme colonne poreuse en trois dimensions, où chaque surface est constituée d'une structure ‹ en sommier › d'éléments de différentes densités découpés au laser dans la tôle d'acier. Tous les panneaux sont en styrofoam (servant à la fois de forme et d'isolant) recouvert de lamifié de fibre de verre époxy à finition métallisée de couleur marron. Les panneaux sont disposés en chevron qui, avec le nervurage renforcé de chaque panneau et la double incurvation de la structure, confèrent au bâtiment un aspect extrêmement sensuel, unique dans le paysage architectural néerlandais. »

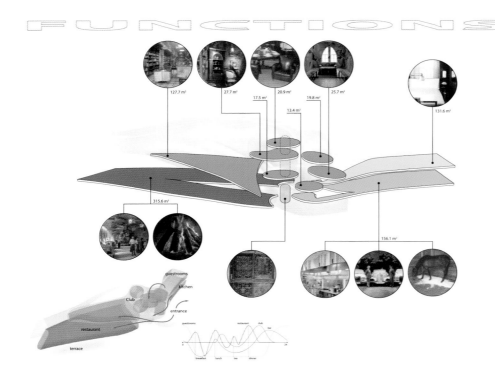

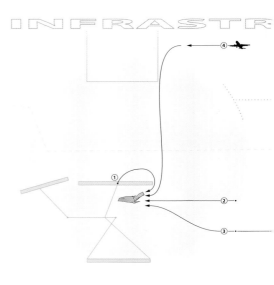

Mixing reassuring old-style clubhouse images with rather surprising computer-generated contemporary shapes, Lars Spuybroek obviously intends to show that his design is not as far from the desired functionality as it might seem.

Mit einer Mischung aus vertrauter Clubhaus-optik alten Stils und eher überraschenden, computergenerierten zeitgenössischen Formen will Lars Spuybroek offenbar zeigen, dass sein Entwurf sich nicht so weit von der gewünschten Funktionalität entfernt, wie es scheint.

En mélangeant des images de clubhouse à l'ancienne à des formes contemporaines de synthèse, Lars Spuybroek veut montrer que son projet n'est pas aussi éloigné du fonctionnalisme souhaité que l'on pourrait le penser.

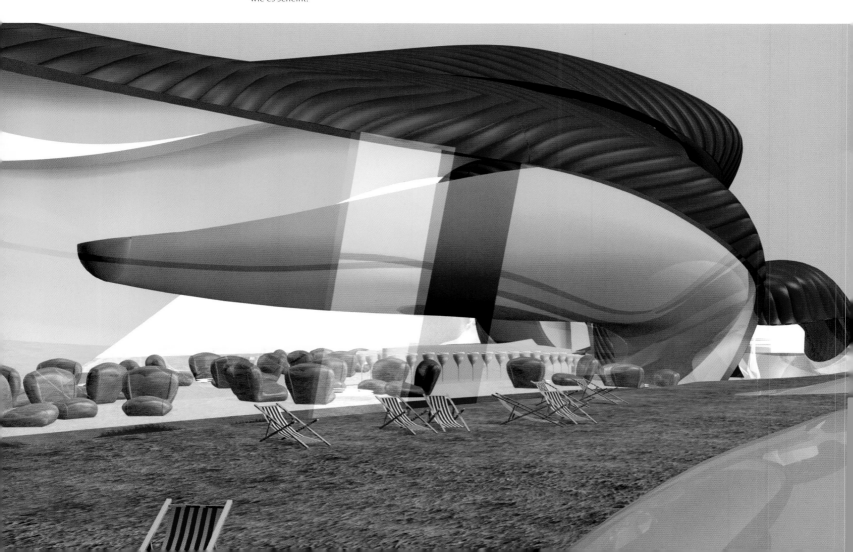

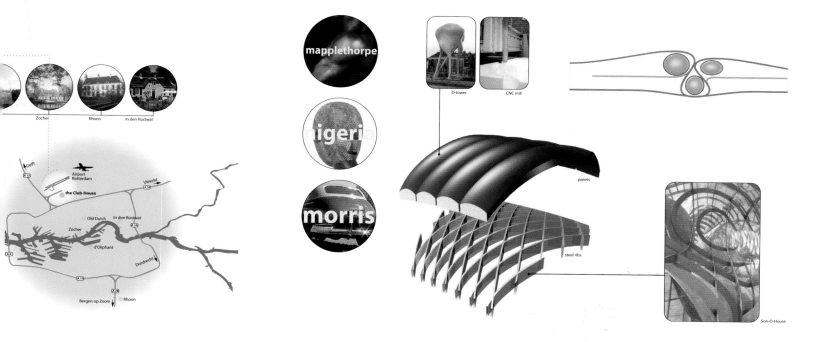

Showing references ranging from abdominal muscles to automobile design, the architect again demonstrates that his work fits into a familiar universe of images and structural designs.

Mit Referenzbildern, die von Bauchmuskeln bis hin zum Automobildesign reichen, hat der Architekt einmal mehr bewiesen, dass seine Werke in einer vertrauten Bild- und Konstruktionswelt verwurzelt sind.

À travers des références qui vont des muscles abdominaux à la conception d'automobiles, l'architecte montre que son travail s'intègre à son univers familier d'images et de projets structurels.

HUNK YOUTH CENTERS
VARIOUS LOCATIONS 2005

FLOOR AREA: 360–560 m²
CLIENT: Vitri Management
COST: €450 000–650 000

Working with Vitri Management, Lars Spuybroek imagined Youth Centers for different cities in the Netherlands on the basis of the creation of a brand that he likens to Nike shoes. As he says, "The design of a Nike shoe is ... not a question of one product but a range of products, and mainly of how the degrees of variation are organized. This organization is called *metadesign*, the design of design, which involves a parameterization where the variation of parts is balanced by a reconfiguration of the whole." His idea is to initiate a similar coordination or system of possible variants for youth centers based on a core brand image. "For the generic building system," explains Spuybroek, "we have chosen a shed typology, a simple hall that is based on the analysis of the program. Within the average size of a small youth center being around 450 m² some 75 % of the program would always be the same for any site: office spaces, event spaces, support program. The other 25 % would always be different. The shed's architecture is crucial, when too conscious and finished it wouldn't interest any local youth, when too peripheral and shabby it would be unacceptable to the neighborhood. The design is based on a steel system making up an initial hall of 12 by 30 meters with portals every 4.8 meters: an industrial typology that allows for contemporary, post-industrial variations, either directly in the structural system itself or as additions." On the basis of this standardized system, the architect has devised a series of possible variants that he assimilates into strategies as opposed to "catalogues." He calls these the "uni," "multi" or "pluri" matrices, which range from a simple, closed configuration to a totally open one "negotiated" with young people who will use the centers.

In Zusammenarbeit mit Vitri Management entwickelte Lars Spuybroek Jugendhäuser für verschiedene Städte, ausgehend von der Kreation eines Markenkonzepts, das er mit Nike-Sportschuhen verglich. „Beim Entwurf eines Nike-Schuhs", sagt er, „geht es nicht um ein einziges Produkt, sondern um eine ganze Produktreihe und v. a. darum, wie Variationen angelegt werden. Diese Methode nennt man *Metadesign*. Sie bezeichnet das Gestalten der Gestaltung und erfordert die Definition von Entwurfsparametern, wobei die Variierung der Einzelteile von der Neugestaltung des Ganzen ausgeglichen wird." Ihm kam daher die Idee, für die Jugendhäuser ähnliche Koordinaten oder ein System möglicher Varianten auf der Basis eines „Brand Image" zu entwickeln. Spuybroek erklärt dazu: „Als Grundtyp des Bausystems wählten wir, nachdem wir das Raumprogramm analysiert hatten, den einfachen Hallentyp. Bei der Größe des üblichen kleinen Jugendhauses mit rund 450 m² wären etwa 75 % der Räume für jeden Standort gleich – Büros, Veranstaltungssäle, Sanitär- und Nebenräume – und 25 % veränderbar. Die archi-

tektonische Gestaltung der Halle ist entscheidend. Allzu stilvoll und ‚geleckt' würde sie die Jugendlichen vertreiben; bewusst schräg und schäbig würde sie von den Nachbarn abgelehnt. Der Entwurf sieht für einen ersten Hallenbau von 12 x 30 m Grundfläche ein Stahltragwerk mit Portalrahmen in Abständen von 4,8 m vor. Dieser Fabrikbautyp ermöglicht zeitgenössische postindustrielle Variationen in der Halle oder die Erweiterung durch Anbauten." Aus diesem Standardsystem leitete der Architekt eine Reihe von Varianten ab, die er in „Strategien" und nicht „Serien" einteilt, bzw. als „Uni-", „Multi-" oder „Plurimatritzen" bezeichnet. Diese reichen von der schlichten geschlossenen Bauform bis hin zur total offenen, die er in „Verhandlungen" mit den Jugendlichen entwickelt, die das jeweilige Zentrum nutzen werden.

En collaboration avec Vitri Management, Lars Spuybroek a imaginé des centres pour jeunes destinés à diverses villes néerlandaises, conçus un peu comme une marque qu'il compare à celle des chaussures Nike. « La conception d'une chaussure Nike ... n'est pas le problème d'un produit, mais d'une gamme de produits et principalement de la façon dont les variantes sont organisées. Cette organisation est appelée *metadesign*, la conception de la conception, qui implique une paramétrisation dans laquelle la variation de parties est équilibrée par la reconfiguration de l'ensemble. » Son idée est d'initier une coordination similaire ou un système de variantes possibles pour des clubs de jeunes à partir d'une image de marque commune. « Pour le système de construction générique, nous avons choisi à partir de l'analyse du programme une typologie de shed, un simple hall. Partant d'une surface moyenne pour ce genre de club de 450 m² environ, 75 % du programme sont identiques partout : bureaux, espace pour les sports, programme de soutien. Les autres 25 % par contre sont toujours différents. L'architecture de shed est cruciale. Une architecture trop soignée trop bien finie n'intéresserait pas les jeunes, trop décalée et trop décontractée elle serait inacceptable par le voisinage. La conception repose sur une structure en acier constituant un premier hall de 12 x 30 m soutenu par des portiques tous les 4,80 m, typologie industrielle qui permet des variantes d'esprit contemporain et post-industriel, que ce soit directement dans le système structurel ou en tant qu'extension. » Sur la base de ce système standardisé, l'architecte a imaginé une série de variantes qu'il assimile à des stratégies, par opposition au simple « catalogue ». Il les appelle des uni-, multi- ou pluri-matrices qui vont d'une configuration fermée simple à d'autres totalement ouvertes « négociées » avec les jeunes utilisateurs.

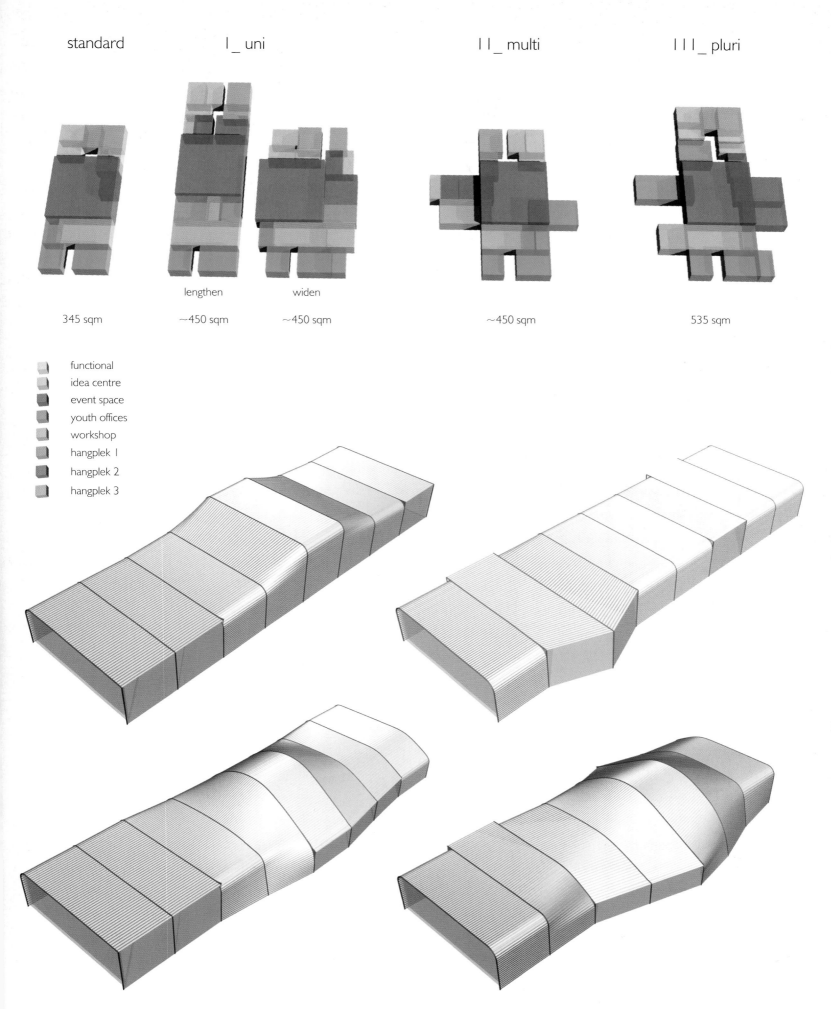

standard

I_ uni

II_ multi

III_ pluri

lengthen

widen

345 sqm

~450 sqm

~450 sqm

~450 sqm

535 sqm

functional
idea centre
event space
youth offices
workshop
hangplek 1
hangplek 2
hangplek 3

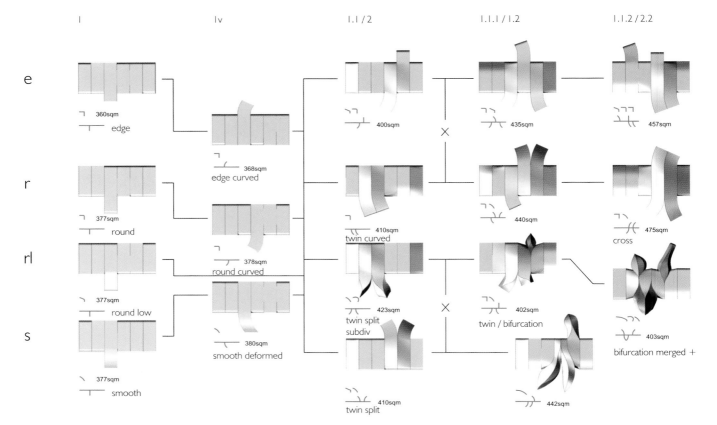

I	Iv	1.1 / 2	1.1.1 / 1.2	1.1.2 / 2.2

e
360sqm
edge

368sqm
edge curved

400sqm

435sqm

457sqm

r
377sqm
round

410sqm
twin curved

440sqm

475sqm
cross

rl
377sqm
round low

378sqm
round curved

423sqm
twin split
subdiv

402sqm
twin / bifurcation

403sqm
bifurcation merged +

s
377sqm
smooth

380sqm
smooth deformed

410sqm
twin split

442sqm

By adding or subtracting various elements, these drawings demonstrate the potential evolution or variations on a theme that can be derived from the basic formula proposed.

Durch Hinzufügen oder Weglassen verschiedener Elemente demonstrieren diese Zeichnungen mögliche Weiterentwicklungen beziehungsweise Variationen der grundlegenden Entwurfsidee.

En ajoutant ou en supprimant certains éléments, ces dessins illustrent l'évolution potentielle ou les variations thématiques que l'on peut tirer de la formule de base.

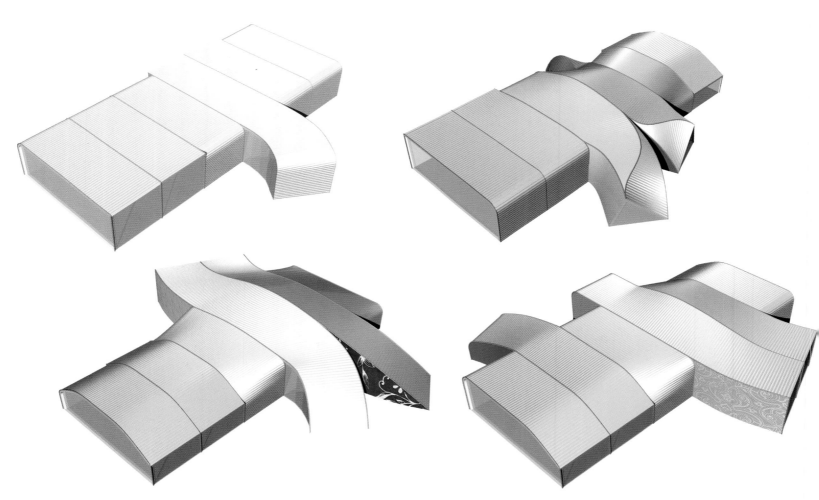

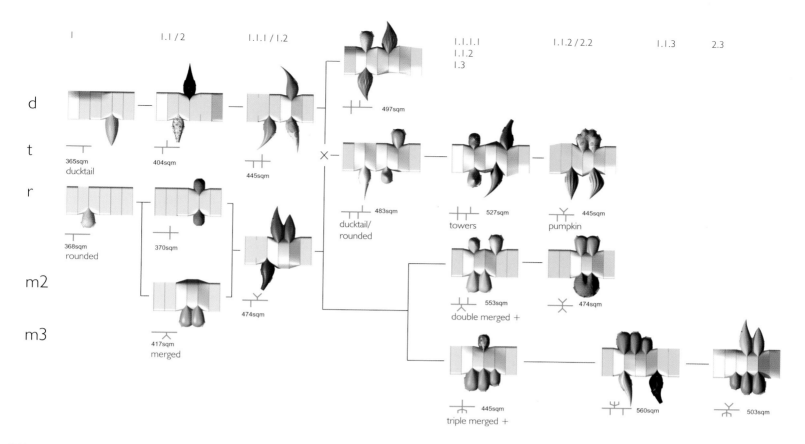

| | | I | 1.1 / 2 | 1.1.1 / 1.2 | | 1.1.1.1 1.1.2 1.3 | 1.1.2 / 2.2 | 1.1.3 | 2.3 |

d

t

365sqm
ducktail

404sqm

445sqm

497sqm

r

368sqm
rounded

370sqm

474sqm

483sqm
ducktail/
rounded

527sqm
towers

445sqm
pumpkin

m2

417sqm
merged

553sqm
double merged +

474sqm

m3

445sqm
triple merged +

560sqm

503sqm

With ornamental patterns on their surfaces, the added elements shown in these drawings are intended to demonstrate the practicality of the system, but they also point the way to an increasingly decorative style in contemporary architecture, whose "minimalist" period is now for the most part over.

Die hier dargestellten Zusatzelemente belegen die Anwendungsmöglichkeiten des Bausystems. Mit ihren Oberflächenornamenten zeugen sie auch vom zunehmend dekorativen Stil der zeitgenössischen Architektur.

Décorés de motifs ornementaux, des éléments ajoutés illustrent l'aspect pratique du système mais témoignent également d'un style décoratif de plus en plus présent dans une architecture contemporaine qui se détache rapidement de sa période « minimaliste ».

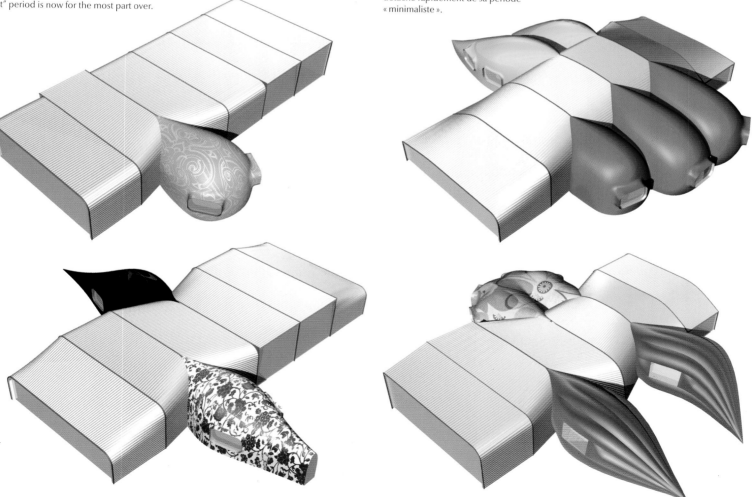

OMA / REM KOOLHAAS

8

OFFICE FOR METROPOLITAN ARCHITECTURE
Heer Bokelweg 149
3032 AD Rotterdam

Tel: +31 10 2 43 82 00
Fax: +31 10 2 43 82 02
e-mail: office@oma.nl
Web: www.oma.nl

REM KOOLHAAS created the Office for Metropolitan Architecture (OMA) in 1975 together with Elia and Zoe Zenghelis and Madelon Vriesendorp. Born in Rotterdam in 1944, Koolhaas tried his hand as a journalist at the *Haagse Post* and as a screenwriter before studying at the Architectural Association (AA) in London. He became well known after the 1978 publication of his book *Delirious New York*. OMA is led today by four partners, Rem Koolhaas, Ole Scheeren, Ellen van Loon, and Joshua Prince-Ramus. Their built work includes a group of apartments at Nexus World, Fukuoka (1991), and the Villa dall'Ava, Saint-Cloud (1985–91). Koolhaas was named head architect of the Euralille project in Lille in 1988, and has worked on a design for the new Jussieu University Library in Paris. His 1400 page book *S,M,L,XL* (Monacelli Press, 1995) has more than fulfilled his promise as an influential writer. He won the 2000 Pritzker Prize and the 2003 Praemium Imperiale Award for Architecture. More recent work of OMA includes a House, Bordeaux, France (1998); the campus center at the Illinois Institute of Technology; the new Dutch Embassy, Berlin; as well as the Guggenheim Las Vegas and Prada boutiques in New York and Los Angeles. OMA completed the Seattle Public Library in 2004, and participated in the Samsung Museum of Art (Leeum) in Seoul with Mario Botta and Jean Nouvel. Current work includes the design of OMA's largest project: the 575 000 m² Headquarters and Cultural Center for China Central Television (CCTV) in Beijing; the 1850 seat Porto Concert Hall; and the New City Center for Almere, for which the firm has drawn up the master plan.

BLOK 6 ALMERE 1998 - 2004

FLOOR AREA: 19 135 m²
CLIENT: MAB
COST: €22.6 million

Responsible for the master plan of Almere's city center, OMA also acted as the architect for Blok 6, which contains cinemas (7680 m²); commercial space (a 3260 m² "mega store"); 1100 m² of smaller retail shops; a restaurant (1280 m²); a supermarket (3230 m²); a loading dock and storage area. The construction budget for the complex was €22.6 million. Set between the "entertainment oriented waterfront and the dense shopping carré," Blok 6 extends to an apartment building (Blok 6A, designed by Van Sambeek & Van Veen), and is closely connected with the other areas of the new city center. In an interesting turn of language, the firm qualifies the volume as being divided between "mass and void—the mass containing program outside the architect's control, the void being a volume where a more coherent identity can be orchestrated." OMA rightly points out that both cinemas and retail space tend to change appearance (and architects) at an extremely high rate, making their presence part of an infinitely variable "mass" whose presence inevitably influences the identity and design of Blok 6. The identity is in fact "derived from its organization." As the firm's description would have it, "Since the void is created by the absence of mass (sic), identity is determined by the void's surface. With the flexibility of graphics and information the surface can cope with the rapid obsolescence of shopping environments—infobabble as wallpaper." All of the pedestrian circulation required for the complex has been located "on top of the shopping mass," confirming the insistence of OMA on the division of the city center into coherent layers and indeed illustrating the theoretical outline of the *Harvard Guide to Shopping* (TASCHEN), another book directed by Koolhaas that insists on the omnipresence of shopping as a driving force of architecture.

OMA zeichnet nicht nur verantwortlich für den Masterplan des Almerer Stadtzentrums, sondern entwarf und baute auch Blok 6, der Kinos (7680 m²), Gewerbeflächen (einen 3260 m² großen „Megastore"), 1100 m² Einzelhandelsgeschäfte, Gastronomie (1280 m²), Supermarkt (3230 m²), Anlieferung und Lagerräume umfasst. Das Baubudget für den Komplex betrug 22,6 Millionen Euro. Zwischen der Entertainment-orientierten Uferbebauung und dem stark verdichteten Einkaufs-Carré gelegen, erstreckt sich Blok 6 bis zum Wohnblock Blok 6A von Van Sambeek & Van Veen und hat gute Verbindungen zu den anderen Teilen des neuen Stadtzentrums. Mit einem interessanten Wortspiel beschreibt OMA den Baukörper als unterteilt in „Masse und Hohlraum – die Masse enthält Räume, die der Kontrolle des Architekten entzogen sind; im Hohlraum lässt sich eine einheitlichere Identität orchestrieren". Mit Recht weist OMA darauf hin, dass Kinos wie Läden ihr Erscheinungsbild (und ihre Architekten) meist in extrem schneller Folge wechseln.

Dadurch werden sie zu Bestandteilen einer unendlich variablen „Masse", welche unweigerlich den Charakter und das Design von Blok 6 beeinflusst. Diese Identität ist tatsächlich „von der Gliederung abgeleitet". Wie es in der Beschreibung des Büros weiter heißt, „ist die Identität von der Oberfläche des Hohlraums bestimmt, da dieser durch die Abwesenheit von Masse entsteht. Dank der Flexibilität der Grafiken und der Information kann sich die Oberfläche der Schnelllebigkeit der Einkaufsangebote anpassen - Infogebabbel als Tapete." Alle für den Komplex benötigten Fußgängerverbindungen liegen auf dem „Dach der Shopping-Masse", in Übereinstimmung mit OMAs konsequenter Aufteilung des Stadtzentrums in kohärente Schichten und dem theoretischen Ansatz des *Harvard Guide to Shopping* (TASCHEN), einem anderen Buch unter Koolhaas' Regie, in dem Shopping als die allgegenwärtige Triebkraft der Architektur verstanden wird.

Responsable du plan directeur du centre ville d'Almere, OMA est également l'architecte du Blok 6 qui regroupe des cinémas (7680 m²), des espaces commerciaux (dont un mégastore de 3260 m²), des boutiques (1100 m²), un restaurant (1280 m²), un supermarché (3230 m²) et des espaces de stockage. Le budget de construction s'est élevé à 22,6 millions d'euros. Implanté entre « la rive, orientée vers les loisirs et le quartier commercial très dense », le Blok 6 voisine avec un immeuble résidentiel (Blok 6A, conçu par van Sambeek & van Veen) et se trouve en connexion directe avec les autres parties du nouveau centre ville. Dans une intéressante manipulation conceptuelle, l'agence décrit le volume comme divisé entre « la masse et le vide, la masse contenant les éléments programmatiques non contrôlés par l'architecte, le vide étant un volume où l'on pouvait orchestrer une identité plus cohérente ». OMA fait remarquer à juste titre que les deux cinémas et les espaces commerciaux tendent à changer d'aspect (et d'architectes) à une vitesse élevée, ce qui fait qu'ils relèvent d'une « masse » infiniment variable dont la présence influe inévitablement sur l'identité et la conception du Blok 6. L'identité, en fait, « dérive de son organisation ... Comme le vide est généré par l'absence de masse (sic), l'identité est déterminée par la surface du vide. À travers la souplesse offerte par les éléments graphiques et d'information, la surface peut s'adapter à l'obsolescence rapide des environnements commerciaux - comme un papier peint. » Toutes les circulations piétonnières se trouvent « au-dessus de la masse commerciale », illustrant l'insistance d'OMA sur la division du centre ville en couches cohérentes et les propos théoriques du *Harvard Guide to Shopping* (TASCHEN), autre ouvrage publié sous la direction de Koolhaas qui insiste sur l'omniprésence de la fonction commerciale en tant que force d'animation de l'architecture.

Though OMA's Blok 6 does not break architectural ground in terms of design, it does offer quality space in circumstances where creativity is normally not at all on the agenda.

Zwar betritt OMA mit Blok 6 kein architektonisches Neuland, der Entwurf bietet aber hohe gestalterische Qualität, obwohl diese bei derartigen Projekten normalerweise keine Priorität hat.

Bien que le Blok 6 d'OMA ne révolutionne pas l'architecture, il offre une qualité de conception remarquable dans des circonstances où l'on n'attend normalement guère de créativité.

Bright colors, large-scale graphics and tilted walls give a feeling of design-consciousness to facilities intended for the general public.

Leuchtende Farben, große Grafiken und schräge Wände bewirken, dass die Architektur für die breite Masse ein gewisses Designbewusstsein ausstrahlt.

Des couleurs vives, des éléments graphiques surdimensionnés et des murs carrelés témoignent d'une sensibilité au design dans des installations destinées au grand public.

SOUTERRAIN THE HAGUE 1999 - 2004

AREA: Tramway tunnel (1250 m),
2 tramway stations, parking garage for
375 cars, poster museum
CLIENT: The City of The Hague,
Projectbureau Tunnels Centrum (PTC)
COST: €234 million

OMA has been involved in a number of projects where transport facilities have to be taken into account, such as the Euralille complex that contains the Lille-Europe TGV station (architect, Jean-Marie Duthilleul) or the more recent McCormick Tribune Campus Center (Illinois Institute of Technology, Chicago, 2000–03) that contains a reinforced concrete-supported acoustical tube, encased in corrugated stainless steel enveloping 160 meters of existing Chicago Transit Authority elevated commuter train track. In a €234 million project in The Hague, OMA has had to deal with 1250 meters of tramway tunnel, two tramway stations, a parking garage for 375 cars and a poster museum—hardly as glamorous a project as some of their other work. The project does fit in well with Koolhaas' theory that urban density is inevitable, since The Hague has reached the physical limits of its potential expansion. The only choice appears to go up or down and to render the urban tissue more dense. The intent of the tunnel designed by OMA was to act "like a spine connecting the separate 'organs', creating a body of underground connections that serves the city from underneath." According to the architects, "The main challenge of this project was to prove that architecture can have a positive effect when applied to the rigour of transport pragmatism." Adding touches of transparency where opacity could be expected, such as the interface between parking areas and tram stations, OMA relied on an almost total absence of architectural finishes "due to the surprising beauty of rock-like concrete walls, poured in the irregular coast soil of The Hague." Budgetary constraints and a general preference for rough surfaces undoubtedly influenced the finishes as much as the "rock-like beauty" of the concrete, but this project remains interesting as an attempt to improve spaces that have been designed as though they didn't matter.

OMA war an einer Reihe von Projekten beteiligt, in deren Rahmen auch Verkehrsbauten entworfen werden mussten, darunter der Euralille-Komplex mit dem TGV-Bahnhof Lille-Europe (Architekt: Jean-Marie Duthilleul) oder in jüngerer Zeit der McCormick Tribune Campus Center (Illinois Institute of Technology, Chicago, 2000–03), wo die Architekten den bestehenden, 160 m langen aufgeständerten Bahnhof einer Pendlerstrecke der Chicago Transit Authority mit einer schallgedämmten, mit Edelstahlblech verkleideten Röhre auf Stahlbetonstützen umhüllten. Beim Souterrain in Den Haag, das auf Kosten in Höhe von 234 Millionen Euro veranschlagt war, ging es um den Bau von 1250 m Straßenbahntunnel, zwei Straßenbahnhaltestellen, einem Parkhaus für 375 Autos und einem Postermuseum – ein wenig glamouröses Programm für OMA. Das Projekt passt jedoch gut in Koolhaas' Theorie über die Unvermeidbarkeit städtischer Dichte, da Den Haag die Grenzen seiner möglichen Expansion erreicht hat. Das Bauen in die Höhe oder die Tiefe und die Verdichtung des städtischen Gefüges scheinen die einzigen Auswege zu sein. Der von OMA entworfene Tunnel soll als „Rückgrat" fungieren, das „die verschiedenen Organe verbindet und ein Netz aus unterirdischen Verbindungen knüpft, das die Stadt von unten her versorgt". Für die Architekten bestand „die größte Herausforderung dieses Projekts [darin] zu beweisen, dass Architektur einen positiven Effekt haben kann, wenn sie auf die strengen, pragmatischen Anforderungen von Verkehrsbauten angewandt wird". OMA fügte einen Hauch von Transparenz hinzu, wo man Undurchsichtigkeit erwarten würde, etwa an der Schnittstelle zwischen Parkhaus und Bahnstation, und verzichtete „aufgrund der überraschenden Schönheit felsengleicher, in den ungleichmäßigen Küstengrund Den Haags gegossener Betonwände" auf Oberflächenveredelung. Ein knappes Budget und die generelle Vorliebe für raue Oberflächen waren dafür zweifellos ebenso entscheidend wie „die felsengleiche Schönheit" des Betons. Dennoch bleibt dieses Projekt interessant, da es den Versuch darstellt, die Qualität von Räumen zu verbessern, deren Gestaltung bislang meist zweitrangig war.

OMA est déjà intervenu sur un certain nombre de projets impliquant les moyens de transport. Ce fut le cas d'Euralille qui englobe la gare TGV Lille-Europe (architecte Jean-Marie Duthilleul) ou le McCormick Tribune Campus Center (Illinois Institute of Technology, Chicago, 2000–03) marqué par un tube acoustique de 160 m en béton armé recouvert d'une gaine d'acier inoxydable dans lequel passent sur une voie surélevée les trains de banlieue. Dans ce projet de 234 millions d'euros pour La Haye, OMA devait prendre en compte un tunnel de tramway de 1250 m, deux arrêts de tram, un parking de 375 places et un musée de l'affiche, ensemble un peu moins séduisant que d'autres projets en cours de l'agence. La solution proposée participe de la théorie de Koolhaas selon laquelle la densité urbaine est inévitable, puisque La Haye a atteint les limites physiques de son potentiel d'expansion. Le seul choix semble de construire au-dessus ou au-dessous et de densifier le tissu urbain. Le tunnel conçu doit jouer le rôle « d'une colonne vertébrale reliant des ‹ organes › séparés, créer un corps de connexions souterraines qui desservent les fonctions de la ville par en dessous ». Selon les architectes : « Le principal défi de ce projet était de prouver que l'architecture pouvait exercer un effet positif lorsqu'on l'appliquait à la rigueur du pragmatisme des transports. » En ajoutant quelques touches de transparence là où l'on attendait l'opacité, OMA a opté pour une absence quasi totale de finition architecturale « face à la beauté surprenante des murs de béton, coulés dans le sol sableux de La Haye, qui évoquent la roche ». Les contraintes budgétaires et la préférence pour les surfaces brutes ont certainement influencé ces finitions au moins autant que la « beauté de rocher » du béton, mais ce projet demeure une intéressante tentative d'améliorer des espaces que l'on concevait jusqu'à présent comme s'ils n'avaient pas d'importance.

If one area is even less likely to harbor good design than shopping centers, it may well be the subways. OMA takes on an even more substantial challenge here than in Almere, and apparently succeeds quite brilliantly.

Wenn es einen Bautyp gibt, bei dem gute Architektur noch seltener ist als bei Einkaufszentren, dann wahrscheinlich bei U-Bahnhöfen. OMA hat sich hier einer noch größeren Herausforderung gestellt als in Almere und eine brillante Lösung geliefert.

S'il existe un domaine qui semble moins ouvert au good design qu'un centre commercial, le métro est probablement celui-ci. OMA a relevé ici avec beaucoup de brio un défi encore plus difficile qu'à Almere.

The visual lines of the Souterrain are not cluttered with useless signage or advertising, which allows the architecture to speak for itself, sober and efficient.

Die ästhetische Linienführung des Souterrain wird nicht von nutzlosen Hinweisschildern oder Reklameelementen verstellt, so dass die Architektur für sich selbst sprechen kann – klar und funktional.

Les perspectives du Souterrain ne sont pas encombrées de publicité ou de signalétique inutile. L'espace architectural s'exprime de lui-même, sobre et efficace.

Few if any architectural firms of the reputation of OMA have dared to venture into the "underworld" constituted by the subways, although France's Jean-Marie Duthilleul (AREP) has also done so in the Paris RER.

Wenn überhaupt haben nur wenige Architekturbüros mit einem ähnlichen Ruf wie OMA sich in die „Unterwelt" des U-Bahnhofsbaus vorgewagt. Eine der wenigen Ausnahmen ist der Franzose Jean-Marie Duthielleul (AREP) mit seinem Pariser RER-Bahnhof.

Pratiquement aucune agence de la réputation d'OMA n'a osé s'aventurer dans le monde souterrain du métro, bien que Jean-Marie Duthilleul et son agence ARPE l'aient fait pour le RER parisien.

#9

ONL

ONL [Oosterhuis_Lénárd]
Essenburgsingel 94c
3022 EG Rotterdam

Tel: +31 10 2 44 70 39
Fax: +31 10 2 44 70 41
e-mail: oosterhuis@oosterhuis.nl
Web: www.oosterhuis.nl

ONL is described as a "multidisciplinary architectural firm where architects, visual artists, web designers and programmers work together and join forces." **KAS OOSTERHUIS** was born in Amersfoort in 1951. He studied architecture at the Technical University in Delft (1970–79) and was a Unit Master at the Architectural Association (AA) in London in 1987–89. He has been a Professor at the Technical University in Delft since 2000. He is a member of the board of the Witte de With Art Center in Rotterdam. He has built the Multimedia Pavilion North Holland, Floriade (2000–01); Headquarters for True Colors, Utrecht (2000–01); and the Salt Water Pavilion Neeltje Jans, Zeeland (1994–97). **ILONA LÉNÁRD** is the other principal of ONL. A visual artist, she was born in Hungary, she lives and worked in the Atelier Theo van Doesburg in Meudon, France (1988-98). She has worked with Kas Oosterhuis an various projects that involve a fusion of art and architecture. One notable recent project is the WTC 911, which project that proposes a "self-executable and programmable hi-res building which reconfigures its shape, content, and character during one year of its life cycle." Other recent work includes: 9 Variomatic catalogue houses, Deventer (2000); TT monument, Assen (2000); and an Acoustic Barrier, Leidsche Rijn, Utrecht (2002). ONL has recently worked on a number of other projects. Their Flyotel, Dubai, is in the design phase and Oosterhuis has also worked on sophisticated projects that use engineering or game software to develop new types of space. ONL's "Protospace" project at the Technical University of Delft involves creating virtual, interactive architecture.

ACOUSTIC BARRIER
LEIDSCHE RIJN
UTRECHT, 2000 - 05

AREA: 1.5-km long acoustic barrier, total surface 10 000 m²; Cockpit building total floor area 8000 m²
CLIENT: Projectbureau Leidsche Rijn Utrecht
COST: Acoustic Barrier: €5 million, including foundations and light program
Cockpit: total €6.4 million, including installations and interior finishings

The 1.5-kilometer-long acoustic barrier located on the A2 highway includes 5000 m² of industrial space. Integrated into the barrier's long curved form is the Hessing Cockpit, intended for the display and sale of Rolls Royce, Bentley, Lamborghini and Maserati cars. Interested in computer design and games, Kas Oosterhuis describes the Cockpit as being "inspired by the cockpit as an integral part of the smooth body of a Starfighter." Using parametric design, which permits an integration of the design and production process, the architects created the Acoustic Barrier with literally thousands of unique parts, all conceived and manufactured with computers. The Barrier itself is described by Oosterhuis as being made up of "long continuous lines. Lines, which do not have an explicit beginning and not an abrupt end." The complex also includes two buildings designed for the BMW dealer Ekris. Conceived like two curving headlights on the BMW 1 and 5 series cars, these buildings, too, are examples of what a recent Centre Pompidou exhibition called "Architectures Non Standard." As Oosterhuis puts it, "The principles of Mass-Customization [MC] and the unique F2F [file to factory] production processes as developed by ONL guarantee that the quality, precision and the costs are close to standard." The "non standard" concept in fact means that architects are freed to design and give direct orders to manufacture unique parts for their buildings and are no longer economically constrained to employ identical structural elements throughout. The whole Acoustic Barrier with its showrooms is undoubtedly innovative and both aesthetically and functionally surprising. Oosterhuis writes, "We decided ... to streamline the concept by looking at our design in a telescopic perspective. We have studied the splines of cars, powerboats and jet planes which are streamlined to diminish drag. Along the A2 highway, the acoustic barrier and the industrial buildings themselves do not move but they are placed aside a continuous stream of cars passing by. The stream of cars flows at a speed of 120 km/h along the acoustic barrier. As a consequence we decided that the proportions of the built volume immersed in the acoustic dike should be boldly stretched along the length of the dike."

In die 1,5 km lange Schallschutzwand an der Autobahn A2 ist ein 5000 m² großer Gewerberaum integriert. Im langen, geschwungenen Wall liegt wie eine Verdickung das Hessing Cockpit, ein Verkaufsausstellungsraum für Luxusautos (Rolls Royce, Bentley, Lamborghini, Maserati). Kas Oosterhuis beschäftigt sich mit Computerdesign und -spielen und beschreibt seinen Entwurf als „vom Cockpit als wesentlichem Element im glatten, eleganten Körper eines Starfighters inspiriert". Bei der Planung der Schallschutzwand bediente der Architekt sich parametrischer Designtechniken, die die Integration von Entwurfs- und Herstellungsprozess ermöglichen, und komponierte das Bauwerk aus Tausenden von Segmenten, die dann computergesteuert gefertigt wurden. Die Schallschutzbarriere besteht laut Oosterhuis aus „langen Linien ohne ausdrücklichen Anfang oder abruptes Ende". Der Komplex umfasst außerdem zwei für den BMW-Händler Ekris entworfene Gebäude. Diese in Anlehnung an zwei Scheinwerfer der 1er- und 5er-Serie von BMW entwickelten Baukörper sind Beispiele dessen, was kürzlich in der Ausstellung „Architectures Non Standard" (nicht genormte Architektur) im Centre Pompidou gezeigt wurde. Oosterhuis stellt fest, dass gemäß den

Prinzipien der „mass-customization" (MC) und der „F2F" (file to factory – vom Dokument zur Fabrik) dieser von ONL entwickelte Herstellungsprozess „annähernd standardisierte Qualität, Präzision und Kosten garantiert". Das „nicht genormte" Design bedeutet in der Tat, dass die Architekten frei gestalten sowie unübliche Bauteile in Auftrag geben können und nicht mehr gezwungen sind, wegen der geforderten Wirtschaftlichkeit serielle Bauelemente einzusetzen. Die Schallschutzwand mit integrierten Ausstellungsräumen ist innovativ und überrascht sowohl in ihrer Ästhetik als auch in ihrer Funktion. Oosterhuis schreibt: „Wir beschlossen, ... den Bau stromlinienförmig zu machen, indem wir das Projekt aus teleskopischer Perspektive betrachteten. Wir studierten verschiedene windschnittig konstruierte Autos, Rennboote und Flugzeuge. Der Schallschutzwall und die Gewerbebauten an der A2 bewegen sich nicht, werden jedoch von einem kontinuierlichen Fahrzeugstrom passiert. Dieser ‚Autostrom' fließt mit einer Geschwindigkeit von 120 km/h vorbei. Das gab für uns den Anstoß, die Proportionen des in den Akustikschutzwall eingebetteten Baukörpers der Länge des Walls entsprechend deutlich in die Länge zu ziehen."

Cette barrière acoustique de 1,5 km de long sur l'autoroute A2 englobe 5000 m² de locaux industriels, dont le Hessing Cockpit, intégré dans la longue forme incurvée et destiné à la présentation et à la vente de Rolls Royce, Bentley, Lamborghini et autres Maserati. Passionné de CAO et de jeux vidéo, Kas Oosterhuis s'est « inspiré du cockpit faisant partie du corps lisse d'un chasseur Starfighter ». Grâce à des modèles paramétriques qui permettent d'intégrer conception et processus de production, les architectes ont créé cette barrière à l'aide de milliers de pièces littéralement uniques, toutes conçues et fabriquées avec l'assistance d'ordinateurs. Selon le descriptif, la barrière se compose de « longues lignes continues ... qui n'ont ni début précis ni fin abrupte ». Le complexe comprend également deux bâtiments conçus pour le concessionnaire BMW Ekris. Dessinés un peu comme les phares incurvés des BMW série 1 et 5, ces deux constructions sont un exemple de ce qu'une récente exposition du Centre Pompidou appelait « l'architecture non standard ». Pour Oosterhuis, « les principes de mass-customization (MC) et des processus de production F2F (File to factory, du fichier à l'usine) développés par ONL font que la qualité, la précision et les coûts sont proches des critères standard en vigueur. » Le concept de « non-standard » signifie en fait que les architectes sont libres de concevoir et de passer directement les commandes de fabrication des pièces uniques nécessaires, sans être économiquement contraints à utiliser des éléments structurels identiques. Ce projet de barrière acoustique et de show-rooms est à la fois novateur et surprenant aussi bien sur le plan esthétique que fonctionnel. Pour Oosterhuis : « Nous avons décidé ... d'épurer le concept en regardant nos plans selon une perspective télescopique. Nous avons étudié les profils de voitures, de bateaux et d'avions qui sont affinés pour réduire les résistances. Le long de l'autoroute A2, la barrière acoustique et les bâtiments industriels ne se déplacent certes pas mais sont disposés le long d'un flux continu de voitures. Ce flux s'écoule à une vitesse de 120 km/h, c'est pourquoi nous avons décidé que les proportions des volumes bâtis immergés dans cette digue acoustique devaient se dilater très franchement le long de celle-ci. »

Kas Oosterhuis and ONL have used parametric modeling, non-standard design and a strong sense of motion or speed to fashion the Acoustic Barrier and Cockpit automobile display building. Use of such advanced techniques has been rare on this scale until now.

Kas Oosterhuis und ONL haben sich bei der Gestaltung der Lärmschutzwand und des „Cockpit"-Ausstellungsraums parametrischer Entwurfstechniken und ‚nicht-genormten Designs' bedient und dem Bauwerk ein starkes Gefühl von Dynamik oder Geschwindigkeit verliehen. Diese fortschrittlichen Techniken wurden bisher nur selten in solchem Ausmaß angewandt.

Kas Oosterhuis et ONL ont fait appel à la modélisation paramétrique, à la conception non-standard et à leur sens affirmé du mouvement ou de la vitesse pour mettre en forme cette barrière acoustique et le show-room d'automobiles « Cockpit ». L'utilisation de techniques aussi avant-gardistes reste rare à cette échelle.

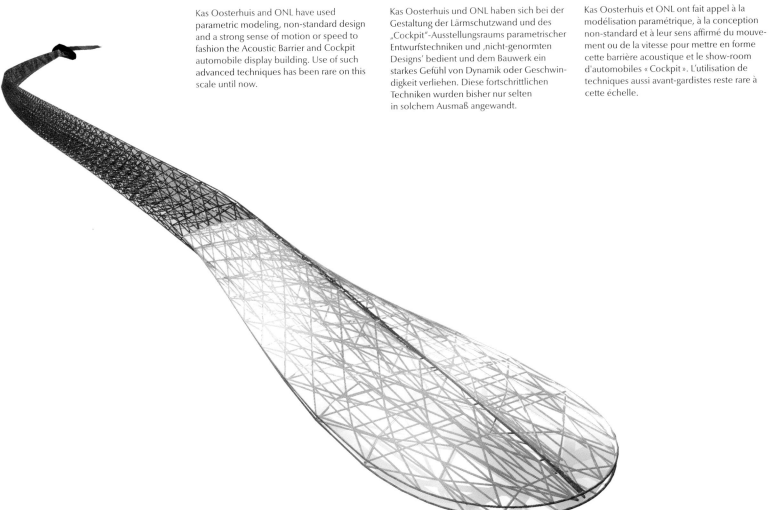

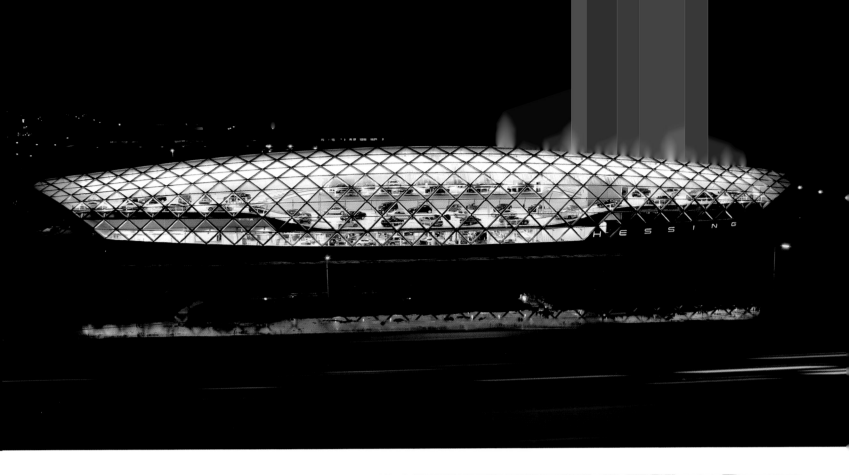

#10

DIRK JAN POSTEL

KRAAIJVANGER · URBIS
Watertorenweg 336
3006 AA Rotterdam

Tel: +31 10 4 98 92 92
Fax: +31 10 4 98 92 00
e-mail: mail@kraaijvanger.urbis.nl
Web: www.kraaijvangerurbis.nl

DIRK JAN POSTEL, born in 1957, graduated in architecture from the Technical University of Delft in 1986. Since 1992, he has been an associate of Kraaijvanger · Urbis, office for architecture and urban design. He is a visiting tutor at the Technical University of Delft, and in the Departments of Architecture and Civil Engineering at Queens College, Belfast; the Bath School of Architecture; the Birmingham School of Architecture; and the University of Central England, Birmingham. He is also the cofounder of GCI, a company for glass consulting and innovation. His work includes: Town Hall, 's-Hertogenbosch (featured here, 1997–2004); Theater, Alphen aan den Rijn (1999–2005); the Temple de l'Amour II, Burgundy, France (2000–01); The British School in the Netherlands, Voorschoten (1999–2003); Traffic Control Center, Dutch Ministry of Transport, Utrecht (1998–2000); Bonhoeffer College, Castricum High School, Castricum (1998–2000); The British School in the Netherlands, The Hague (1994–97); "De Barones" shopping arcade, department store and housing in the center of Breda (with CZWG architects, 1993–97); The Glass House, Almelo (1996–97); and The Glass Bridge, Rotterdam (1993–94).

TOWN HALL
's-HERTOGENBOSCH
1998 - 2004

FLOOR AREA: 21 142 m²
CLIENT: The Municipality of 's-Hertogenbosch
COST: €35 million

Generally known to the Dutch as Den Bosch, 's-Hertogenbosch means "the woods of the Duke," after Henry I of Brabant, who gave the city its rights and trading privileges in 1185. Originally a walled city, Den Bosch is located 95 kilometers south of Amsterdam in the province of North Brabant, and has a population of 133 000 (2004). It has a rich history, a number of important old buildings, like the Sint Janskathedraal, and was the city of the painter Hieronymus Bosch (c. 1450–1516). Dirk Jan Postel's new town hall for 's-Hertogenbosch has two main components: the city offices and the council chamber, designed as an extension of the existing, monumental town hall. An austere façade of limestone and glass, integrated into the urban block, expresses the council chamber with its prominent function. The much larger city offices are a complex structure, incorporating three existing premises. A total floor area of 21 142 m² was built with a new façade only 25 meters long on the exterior. Inside, as the architect says, "the complex that is defined by a system of voids, and all façades are transparent." Dirk Jan Postel is known as an architect with a fondness for glass, having won the 2002 DuPont Benedictus Award given for the use of laminated glass in construction, for his Temple de l'Amour II (Talus du Temple, Burgundy, France, 2000–01). "The design," says the architect, explaining his work in Den Bosch, "refers to the historically hybrid structure of parcels and courts." A small river called the Dieze runs across the site and is integrated into the plan. The office interiors are modern, and flexible. Desks are activity-related (as opposed to being related to a person), resulting in a more complex and stimulating environment.

Den Niederländern allgemein als Den Bosch bekannt, bedeutet 's-Hertogenbosch „der Wald des Herzogs", so benannt nach Heinrich I. von Brabant, der dem Ort 1185 Stadtrecht und Handelsprivilegien verlieh. Den Bosch, 95 km südlich von Amsterdam in der Provinz Nord-Brabant gelegen, war ursprünglich eine befestigte Stadt und hat heute 133 000 Einwohner (2004). Von der reichen Geschichte zeugen zahlreiche bedeutende Baudenkmäler wie die Sint-Jans-Kathedrale. Hier lebte der Maler Hieronymus Bosch (um 1450–1516). Dirk Jan Postels neues Rathaus für 's-Hertogenbosch besteht aus zwei Hauptkomponenten, dem Bürobau der Stadtverwaltung und einer Erweiterung des denkmalgeschützten Rathauses. Eine nüchterne Fassade aus Kalkstein und Glas, eingefügt in eine städtische Blockbebauung, macht den Ratssaal mit seiner bedeutenden Funktion sichtbar. Das wesentlich größere Bürogebäude ist eine komplexe Struktur, die drei

Altbauten mit einer Gesamtfläche von 21 142 m² innerhalb einer neuen, nur 25 m langen Außenfassade zusammenfasst. Im Inneren, so der Architekt, sind „der durch ein System von Lufträumen gegliederte Komplex und alle Fassaden transparent". Dirk Jan Postel wurde für seine Vorliebe für Glas bekannt, nachdem ihm für den Einsatz von konstruktivem Glaslaminat 2002 der DuPont Benedictus Award für seinen Temple de l'Amour II (Talus du Temple, Burgund, Frankreich, 2000–01) verliehen worden war. „Der Entwurf", erklärt der Architekt seine Arbeit in Den Bosch, „bezieht sich auf die historische Mischstruktur aus Parzellen und Höfen". Das Flüsschen Dieze fließt durch das Baugrundstück und ist in den Entwurf integriert. Die Innenausstattung der Büros ist modern und flexibel. Die Schreibtische sind funktionsbezogen (im Gegensatz zu personenbezogen) ausgestattet und bieten so ein vielfältiges und anregendes Arbeitsumfeld.

'S-Hertogenbosch, ou Bois-le-Duc, tient son nom de Henri Ier de Brabant qui accorda à la cité des droits et privilèges commerciaux en 1185. Jadis entourée de remparts, la ville se trouve à 95 km au sud d'Amsterdam dans la province du Nord Brabant et compte une population de 133 000 habitants (2004). Elle possède une riche histoire, un certain nombre de bâtiments historiques comme la cathédrale Saint-Jean, et fut la résidence du peintre Jérôme Bosch (vers 1450–1516). Le nouvel hôtel de ville édifié par Dirk Jan Postel se compose de deux parties principales : les bureaux et la salle du conseil municipal conçue comme une extension de l'ancien hôtel de ville monumental. Une austère façade de pierre calcaire et de verre intégrée à l'ensemble exprime la fonction éminente de la salle du conseil. Les bureaux occupent un bâtiment beaucoup plus vaste intégrant trois bâtiments existants. Au total, 21 142 m² ont été construits derrière une façade nouvelle de 25 m de long donnant sur l'extérieur. À l'intérieur, l'architecte explique que « le complexe se définit par un système de vides et toutes les façades sont transparentes ». Dirk Jan Postel est connu pour son attachement au verre. Il a, par exemple, remporté le Prix DuPont Benedictus 2002 pour l'utilisation du verre laminé dans son Temple de l'amour II (Talus du Temple, Bourgogne, France, 2000–01). « La conception se réfère à la structure historique hybride de parcelles et de cours. » Une petite rivière, la Dieze, traverse le site et a été intégrée à l'ensemble. L'aménagement des bureaux est moderne et souple. Les plans de travail sont affectés aux tâches (et non aux personnes) ce qui génère un environnement plus complexe et plus stimulant.

Postel's design is cool and airy, allowing for ample natural light and plenty of space for the municipal business of 's-Hertogenbosch.

Postels Bau ist kühl und luftig, von natürlichem Licht durchflutet und bietet viel Platz für sämtliche Funktionen der Stadtverwaltung von 's-Hertogenbosch.

La conception du projet de Postel détendue et aérienne offre à la municipalité de 's-Hertogenbosch des volumes généreux baignés d'une abondante lumière naturelle.

Angled walkways enliven what might
otherwise be a relatively ordinary, if
generously proportioned, passageway.

In Winkeln angelegt Brückenstege beleben
eine ansonsten recht gewöhnliche,
wenn auch breite Passage.

Des passerelles inclinées animent ce qui
n'aurait pu rester qu'un hall de proportions
généreuses mais de présence relativement
ordinaire.

#11

SEARCH

SeARCH
Hamerstraat 3
1021 JT Amsterdam

Tel: +31 20 7 88 99 00
e-mail: search@bjarnemastenbroek.nl
Web: www.searcharchitects.nl

SeARCH is a new architecture office, established in Amsterdam in 2002 by Bjarne Mastenbroek (born 1964) and Ad Bogerman (born 1965). Together with Dick van Gameren, Mastenbroek won the Europan II competition in 1991 and created Van Gameren-Mastenbroek Architects. This office merged with De Architectengroep in 1993. Mastenbroek worked on the Dutch Embassy in Addis Ababa (1998–2004); Triade, the conversion and extension of a cultural education center, Den Helder (1997–2001); Bredero College, extension to a trade school, Amsterdam Noord (1998–2001); and buildings in Lelystad and Almere. As the firm description would have it, "SeARCH consists of about twenty international architects and staff members who develop architecture, urbanism and landscaping and conduct research into new building products and materials. SeARCH develops its concepts in collaboration with designers from other disciplines to create original and unusual design solutions."

POSBANK TEA PAVILION
RHEDEN
1998 - 2002

FLOOR AREA: 760 m²
CLIENT: Vereniging Natuurmonumenten, 's-Gravezand
COST: €1.4 million

Bjarne Mastenbroek completed this project working with his former firm De Architectengroep. Working for the Dutch Nature Conservancy (Vereniging Natuurmonumenten), the architect was given the mission to build "a natural restaurant in a natural environment," but he immediately counters that this is precisely what he did not do. Looking at the site, he says, "Two hundred years ago this was farmland; before that it was a forest, and it's a forest again today. Its 'natural' environment is not only manufactured, but also, to a certain extent, kitsch, except for the elevations. The experience of nature is already artificial. The design is about the schizophrenic idea that a nature organization would build something. It is a building that aims a sly wink at naturalness." The supporting wood struts are real oak tree trunks with the bark removed, but the "boulders" that dot the building are fakes created by an American rock-mold maker and they conceal structural elements. Floors are covered with two centimeter-thick slices of acacia trees set in epoxy. The building has no right angles and the entire structure was drawn with three-dimensional-coordinate AutoCad. The Posbank Pavilion was one of the four finalists of the AM NAI Prize 2004 for Young Architects.

Bjarne Mastenbroek erarbeitete dieses Projekt noch im Büro De Architectengroep. Den Auftrag zum Bau eines „naturverbundenen Restaurants in einer natürlichen Umgebung" erteilte ihm der niederländische Naturschutzbund (Vereniging Natuurmonumenten). Mastenbroek betont sofort, dass er genau das nicht getan hat. Er blickt über das Gelände und erklärt: „Vor 200 Jahren war dies Ackerland, davor war es Wald und heute ist es wieder ein Wald. Die ‚natürliche' Umgebung ist demnach nicht nur vom Menschen gemacht, sondern bis auf die ursprüngliche Topografie auch irgendwie kitschig. Schon das Erlebnis dieser Natur ist also künstlich herbeigeführt. Der Entwurf thematisiert den schizophrenen Umstand, dass ein Naturverband etwas bauen möchte. Der Pavillon ist der Versuch, Natür-

lichkeit mit listigem Augenzwinkern zu erzielen." Die tragenden Holzstreben bestehen aus echten Eichenstämmen, von denen die Rinde entfernt wurde; die im Gebäude verteilten „Felsblöcke" sind dagegen Nachbildungen, die von einem amerikanischen Hersteller von Fels-Gussformen angefertigt wurden und hinter denen sich konstruktive Bauteile verbergen. Der Fußbodenbelag besteht aus Epoxidharz, in das 2 cm dicke Akazienholzscheiben eingelegt wurden. Im ganzen Pavillon gibt es keinen rechten Winkel; das Gebäude wurde vollständig mithilfe des räumlichen Koordinatensystems von AutoCAD entworfen. Der Posbank Pavillon gehörte zu den vier Finalisten des AM NAI-Preises 2004 für Junge Architekten.

Bjarne Mastenbroek a achevé son projet alors qu'il travaillait encore pour son ancienne agence De Architectengroep. La mission confiée par le Conservatoire des monuments naturels (Vereniging Natuurmonumenten) était de construire « un restaurant naturel dans un environnement naturel », il précise immédiatement que c'est précisément ce qu'il n'a pas fait. « Il y a deux ans, ce terrain était agricole. Avant c'était une forêt et c'est de nouveau une forêt. Cet environnement ‹ naturel › est en fait une production humaine mais également dans une certaine mesure kitsch, à l'exception des élévations. L'expérience de la nature y est déjà artificielle. La conception traite de cette idée schizophrénique que l'organisation de la nature construit quelque chose. C'est une construction qui adresse un clin d'œil à la notion de nature. » Les poutres de soutien sont de vrais troncs d'arbres dégagés de leur écorce, mais les « rochers » qui parsèment le bâtiment sont des faux créés par un spécialiste américain de fausse rocaille pour dissimuler des éléments structurels. Les sols sont recouverts de ronds d'acacia de 2 cm d'épaisseur pris dans un lit d'époxy. Le bâtiment entièrement dessiné à l'aide d'un logiciel AutoCad ne présente aucun angle droit. Il a figuré parmi les quatre finalistes du Prix des Jeunes architectes AM NAI 2004.

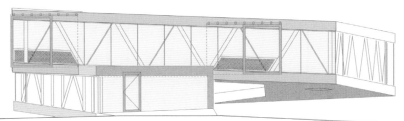

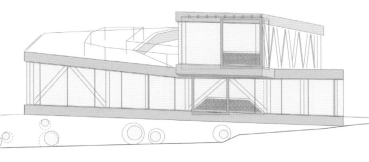

In this pavilion, what appears to be natural is "fake" and vice versa. In any case, the architect has succeeded in giving an impression of being close to nature and has created a space that is very much in contact with its wooded setting.

In diesem Pavillonbau ist alles künstlich, was natürlich erscheint – und umgekehrt. Auf jeden Fall ist es dem Architekten gelungen, den Eindruck von Naturnähe zu erwecken und einen Bau zu schaffen, der sich in seine waldreiche Umgebung einfügt.

Dans ce pavillon, le naturel est « faux » et vice-versa. En tout état de cause, les architectes ont réussi à donner une impression d'être proches de la nature en réalisant un volume en contact étroit avec son cadre boisé.

WOLZAK FARMHOUSE
ZUTPHEN 2002 · 04

FLOOR AREA: 500 m²
CLIENT: not disclosed
COST: not disclosed

For this project, credited to the firm SeARCH, Bjarne Mastenbroek renovated and added to an existing farmhouse and outbuildings. A brief requiring the partial demolition of the T-shaped farmhouse and the construction of a new extension also suggested that workspaces and guestrooms would be located in an adjacent, detached barn. The architect chose to retain the volume of the existing farmhouse for the entire program, replacing a livestock barn, forming the stem of the T-shaped plan with a new structure of similar shape. This extension, made with prefabricated load-bearing wooden panels, contains the entrance, kitchen, workspace and garden shed. The roof and other exterior surfaces of the extension are clad in a "continuous skin of vertical timber laths." The barn, originally intended for the guestrooms, remained "untouched for future development, possibly to be converted into a swimming pool." With these unusual solutions, SeARCH succeeded in intervening on a historically and an aesthetically sensitive environment, where contemporary architecture is often not well received, to the satisfaction of all those concerned.

Bei diesem Projekt von SeARCH handelt es sich um den Umbau und die Erweiterung eines alten Bauernhauses mit Nebengebäuden. Der Bauherr wünschte den teilweisen Abriss des T-förmigen Hauses und einen neuen Anbau sowie den Einbau von Arbeitsräumen und Gästezimmern in eine freistehende Scheune. Der Architekt entschied sich dafür, das Raumvolumen des Altbaus für das gesamte Programm beizubehalten und den Viehstall, der den Längsbalken des alten T-förmigen Grundrisses bildete, durch einen ähnlich geformten neuen Anbau zu ersetzen. Dieser wurde aus vorgefertigten tragenden Holzwänden errichtet und beherbergt nun die Eingangsdiele, die Küche, einen Büro- und einen Gartengeräteraum. Dach und Fassaden des Anbaus sind mit einer „durchgehenden Haut aus vertikalen Holzlatten" verkleidet. Die ursprünglich als Gästehaus vorgesehene Scheune blieb „erst einmal unberührt, um später ausgebaut zu werden, vielleicht zu einem kleinen Schwimmbad". Mit derartigen ungewöhnlichen Lösungen gelang es SeARCH, einen in historischer und gestalterischer Hinsicht sensiblen Bestand – in dem zeitgenössische Architektur häufig nicht gern gesehen ist – zur allseitigen Zufriedenheit zu verändern.

Ce projet a consisté en la rénovation et l'extension d'une ferme et de ses dépendances. Le cahier des charges qui demandait la démolition partielle de la ferme en T et la construction d'une nouvelle extension suggérait également que la zone de travail et les chambres d'amis soient implantées dans une grange adjacente détachée. L'architecte décida de conserver le volume de la maison de ferme existante et de remplacer l'étable formant la tige du plan en T par une structure nouvelle de forme similaire. Cette extension en panneaux de bois porteurs préfabriqués contient l'entrée, la cuisine, un espace de travail et un abri de jardin. Le toit et les façades sont habillés « d'une peau continue de lattes de bois ». La grange, prévue à l'origine pour les chambres d'amis, est « réservée à de futurs développements, peut-être une piscine ». Par ces solutions inhabituelles, SeARCH a réussi son intervention sur un environnement historiquement et esthétiquement sensible qui accepte souvent mal l'architecture contemporaine à la satisfaction de toutes les personnes concernées.

The challenge of using wood and abutting a traditional farmhouse seem to have stimulated the creativity of the architects, who have used a traditional vocabulary to speak a modern language.

Die Herausforderung, ein neues Holzhaus an ein herkömmliches altes Bauernhaus anzubauen, hat offenbar die schöpferische Fantasie der Architekten beflügelt, die hier mit traditionellem Vokabular moderne Architektur geschaffen haben.

Le défi d'avoir à utiliser le bois et de s'ancrer à une ferme traditionnelle semble avoir stimulé la créativité des architectes qui ont emprunté un vocabulaire classique mais dans une expression moderne.

12

UN STUDIO

UN STUDIO, VAN BERKEL & BOS
Stadhouderskade 113
1073 AX Amsterdam

Tel: +31 20 5 70 20 40
Fax: +31 20 5 70 20 41
e-mail: info@unstudio.com
Web: www.unstudio.com

BEN VAN BERKEL was born in Utrecht in 1957 and studied at the Rietveld Academy in Amsterdam and at the Architectural Association (AA) in London, receiving the AA Diploma with honors in 1987. After working briefly in the office of Santiago Calatrava in 1988, he set up his practice in Amsterdam with **CAROLINE BOS**. He has been a visiting professor at Columbia University and a visiting critic at Harvard University (1994). He was a Diploma Unit Master at the AA, London (1994–95). As well as the Erasmus Bridge in Rotterdam (inaugurated in 1996), Van Berkel & Bos Architectural Bureau, now called UN Studio, has built the Karbouw and ACOM (1989–93) office buildings; the REMU electricity station (1989–93), all in Amersfoort; and housing projects and the Aedes East gallery for Kristin Feireiss in Berlin. More recent projects include the Möbius House, Naarden (1993–98); Het Valkhof Museum, Nijmegen (1995–98); an extension of the Rijksmuseum Twente, Enschede (1992–96); a Music Facility, Graz (1998–2002); Switching Station, Innsbruck (1998–2001); NMR Laboratory, Utrecht; the Mercedes Benz Museum, Stuttgart (2002–06); an Electricity Station, Innsbruck; and the Arnhem Station. UN Studio was also a participant in the recent competition for the new World Trade Center in New York, in collaboration with Foreign Office Architects (FOA), Greg Lynn FORM, Imaginary Forces, Kevin Kennon and Reiser + Umemoto, RUR, under the name of United Architects.

LA DEFENSE
ALMERE
1999 - 2004

FLOOR AREA: 23 000 m²
CLIENT: Eurocommerce, Deventer
COST: €32 million

This 23 000 m² office complex is located in the Business Center of the new city of Almere, behind the Central Station. Organized in four separate bands of different lengths and heights (3, 4, 5 or 6 levels), the plan is essentially closed with two openings that connect to a park at the rear of the site. Parking for the complex is located under the buildings, freeing the immediate environment and the inner courtyard of vehicles. A simple metal façade faces out, but numerous entrances allow for La Defense to be used by a large number of different companies. In order to keep rents low, the structure was built on a strict budget (€32 million), which did not prevent the architects from adding one very unusual feature. The inner façade of La Defense changes colors depending on the time of day and the type of light available. The glass used by the architects has a multicolored foil manufactured by 3M called Radiant Color Film integrated into its surface. Usually used on perfume bottles, this foil creates an almost magical light effect within the courtyards of the building. Ben van Berkel's interest in contemporary art and photography led him to this unusual solution, turning what could have been a banal office building into a widely published architectural success. In an interesting play on this creativity, Van Berkel has taken a number of unusual digital pictures of the building that include shadows photographed against the background of the fiery red orange inner façades. Movement and color suddenly animate the often gray Dutch environment.

Dieser Bürokomplex mit 23 000 m² liegt hinter dem Bahnhof im Geschäftsviertel der neuen Stadt Almere. In vier separate Riegel von unterschiedlicher Länge und Höhe (mit drei bis sechs Etagen) aufgeteilt, ist der Grundriss im Wesentlichen geschlossen, bis auf zwei Öffnungen zu einem Park auf der Rückseite. Parkmöglichkeiten für den Komplex befinden sich in den Untergeschossen, dadurch werden die Umgebung und der Innenhof von Fahrzeugen frei gehalten. Die schlichte Außenfassade ist aus Metall. Aufgrund zahlreicher Eingänge kann La Défense von vielen verschiedenen Firmen genutzt werden. Um die Mieten niedrig zu halten, wurde das Gebäude mit einem knappen Budget von 32 Millionen Euro erbaut, was die Architekten nicht daran hinderte, ein höchst originelles Gestaltungsmerkmal

hinzuzufügen. Die Innenfassaden von La Défense wechseln abhängig von Tageszeit und Lichtverhältnissen die Farbe: In die Glasscheiben ist eine mehrfarbige Folie (Radiant Color Film von 3M) eingearbeitet. Diese normalerweise für Parfümflakons verwendete Folie erzeugt „magische" Lichteffekte in den Innenhöfen. Ben van Berkels Interesse an zeitgenössischer Kunst und Fotografie brachte ihn auf diese ungewöhnliche Lösung, die ein andernfalls banales Bürogebäude zu einem weithin publizierten architektonischen Erfolg gemacht hat. Van Berkel hat dazu einige ungewöhnliche digitale Fotografien des Gebäudes aufgenommen, die Schattenspiele auf den feurig orangefarbenen Fassaden zeigen. In die oft graue niederländische Landschaft kommen plötzlich Farbe und Bewegung.

Cet ensemble de bureaux de 23 000 m² est situé dans le quartier d'affaires de la nouvelle ville d'Almere, derrière la gare centrale. Organisé en cinq barres séparées, de longueurs et hauteurs différentes (trois, quatre, cinq ou six niveaux), son plan est fermé mais deux ouvertures le relient à un parc en partie arrière du terrain. Les parkings sont implantés sous les bâtiments pour libérer l'environnement immédiat et les cours de tout véhicule. La façade métallique de conception simple possède de nombreuses entrées adaptées aux besoins de la multiplicité des locataires. Le budget limité (32 millions d'euros) a permis de maintenir des loyers raisonnables mais n'a pas empêché les architectes de créer une surprise visuelle. La façade intérieure change en effet de couleurs en fonction de l'heure du jour et de la lumière. Le verre est recouvert d'un film 3M, le Radiant Color Film – utilisé d'habitude sur les flacons de parfum – pour créer un effet lumineux quasi magique dans la cour des immeubles. L'intérêt de Ben van Berkel pour l'art et la photographie d'aujourd'hui lui a inspiré cette solution pour transformer ce qui n'aurait pu être qu'un immeuble de bureaux banal en une réussite architecturale, amplement médiatisée. Poussant le jeu plus loin, il a pris un certain nombre de photos numériques dont certaines d'ombres photographiées sur le fond rouge orange vif des façades intérieures : le mouvement et la couleur réveillent totalement un environnement hollandais souvent terne.

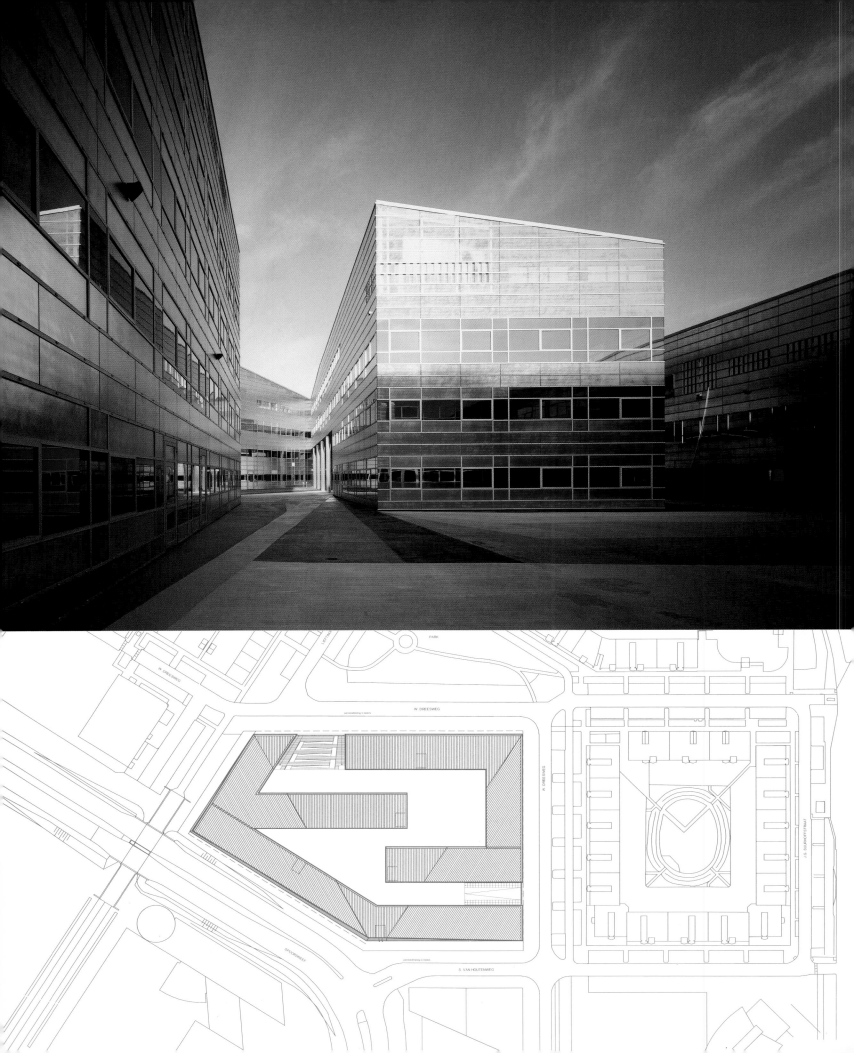

Working on a large scale, Ben van Berkel and UN Studio experiment here with a beauty that is in a sense only skin-deep, since the coloring is a matter of façade, and yet the effect is so strong that the architecture gives off a feeling of well-being.

Ben van Berkel und UN Studio experimentieren hier im großen Maßstab mit oberflächlicher Schönheit. Die farbige Gestaltung beschränkt sich auf die Fassade, verleiht aber dem gesamten Gebäude eine positive Ausstrahlung.

En travaillant à grande échelle, Ben van Berkel et UN Studio ont expérimenté ici une approche de la beauté qui n'est en un sens que de surface puisque la coloration ne concerne que la façade, mais ils ont obtenu un effet si puissant que l'architecture exprime un sentiment de bien-être.

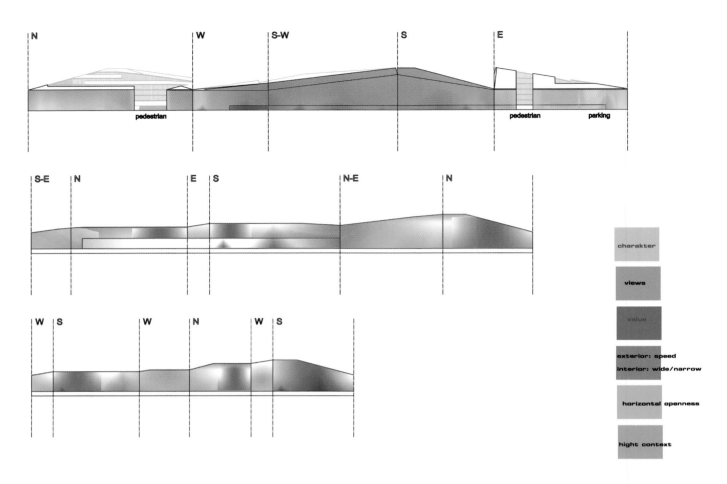

N | W | S-W | S | E

pedestrian | pedestrian | parking

S-E | N | E | S | N-E | N

W | S | W | N | W | S

charakter

views

value

exterior: speed
interior: wide/narrow

horizontal openness

hight context

The film coating on the windows gives a varied effect, according to the angle of the sun and the hour of the day—an original approach to changing appearance in architecture.

Die Filmbeschichtung der Fensterscheiben changiert je nach Sonneneinstrahlungswinkel und Tageszeit – ein origineller Kunstgriff, um das Erscheinungsbild eines Gebäudes zu verändern.

L'application d'un film sur les baies crée un effet varié qui se modifie selon l'orientation du soleil en fonction des heures de la journée, approche originale au changement d'apparence en architecture.

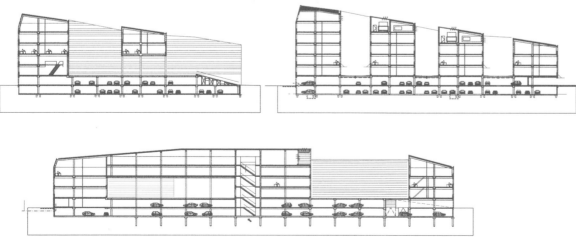

The repetitive massing of the office buildings and the unusual courtyards increase the reflections and color variations, depending on the angle at which they are viewed.

Die regelmäßig gegliederten Bürotrakte und ungewöhnlichen Höfe zeigen je nach Blickwinkel des Betrachters überraschende Spiegelungen und Farbwechsel.

La répartition répétitive des masses des immeubles de bureaux et des cours crée des reflets et des variations de couleur qui dépendent de l'angle sous lequel ils sont regardés.

THEATER
LELYSTAD
2002 - 05

FLOOR AREA: 5890 m²
CLIENT: Municipality of Lelystad
COST: €12.4 million

This theater, with total seating for 925 persons (725 in a large theater hall, 200 in a smaller one), is intended to serve as a beacon in the new city center of Lelystad, whose master plan was laid out by the landscape architects West 8. With its tower visible from the Central Station, it should signal the presence of a vibrant cultural life. Lit at night, the tower is also meant to be seen from various parking facilities located nearby. A vertical foyer connects the different parts of the structure, emphasizing the desire of the architects to "bring the complexity of a multifunctional theater back into a flexible, transparent and intelligent design." As the architects make clear, "UN Studio has worked on different projects where theater art and new media were important aspects in the program. The interaction between different art disciplines should be integrated in the design process of these buildings. UN Studio's expertise lies in the analytical approach of the design requirements. During the research process, before the design process, questions regarding special organization and the multifunctional use of the theater obtain an important role." Set on a 2925 m² site, the theater has a floor area of 5890 m² and a volume of 30 000 m³.

Das Theater verfügt über 925 Sitzplätze, 725 im großen Saal und 200 im kleinen, und setzt ein Signal im Stadtzentrum von Lelystad, dessen Masterplan vom Landschaftsarchitekturbüro West 8 entwickelt wurde. Mit seinem vom Hauptbahnhof aus sichtbaren Turm soll das Theater ein Zeichen für das pulsierende kulturelle Leben in der Stadt setzen. Die Beleuchtung macht ihn auch nachts weiterhin sichtbar. Ein hohes Foyer verbindet die verschiedenen Teile des Gebäudes und betont dadurch den Wunsch des Architekten, „die Vielschichtigkeit dieses multifunktionalen Theaters in einem flexiblen, transparenten und intelligenten Design zu vereinen." Weiter heißt es, dass „UN Studio an verschiedenen

Projekten gearbeitet hat, bei denen Theaterkunst und neue Medien wichtige Aspekte des Raumprogramms waren. Die Wechselwirkung verschiedener gestalterischer Disziplinen sollte in den Entwurfsprozess solcher Gebäude einbezogen werden. Die Stärke von UN Studio liegt in der analytischen Annäherung an die Anforderungen eines Entwurfs. Während des Research-Prozesses, also noch vor dem Designprozess, spielen Fragen zur besonderen Organisation und zum multifunktionalen Gebrauch des Theaters eine wichtige Rolle." Das Theater auf einem 2925 m² großen Grundstück hat eine überbaute Fläche von 5890 m² und einen Gebäudeinhalt von 30 000 m³.

Ce théâtre de 925 places (725 dans la grande salle, 200 dans la petite) devrait devenir l'une des principales attractions du nouveau centre ville de Lelystad dont le plan directeur a été établi par les architectes paysagistes de West 8. Sa tour visible de la gare centrale signale l'existence d'un lieu culturel majeur. Éclairée la nuit elle s'aperçoit également des divers parkings aménagés dans la zone. Un foyer vertical connecte les différentes parties du bâtiment, selon le désir des architectes « d'importer la complexité d'un théâtre multifonctions dans un concept souple, transparent et intelligent ». Comme le fait remarquer l'architecte : « UN Studio a travaillé sur différents projets dans lesquels l'art théâtral et les nouveaux médias constituaient d'importants aspects du programme. L'interaction entre les différentes disciplines artistiques doit être intégrée dans le processus de conception de ce type de bâtiment. L'expertise de UN Studio tient à l'approche analytique des contraintes de conception. Au cours du processus de recherche, avant donc la phase conception, les questions sur les particularités de l'organisation et l'utilisation multifonctionnelle du théâtre ont joué un rôle important. » Sur un terrain de 2925 m², le théâtre offre une surface de 5890 m² pour un volume de 30 000 m³.

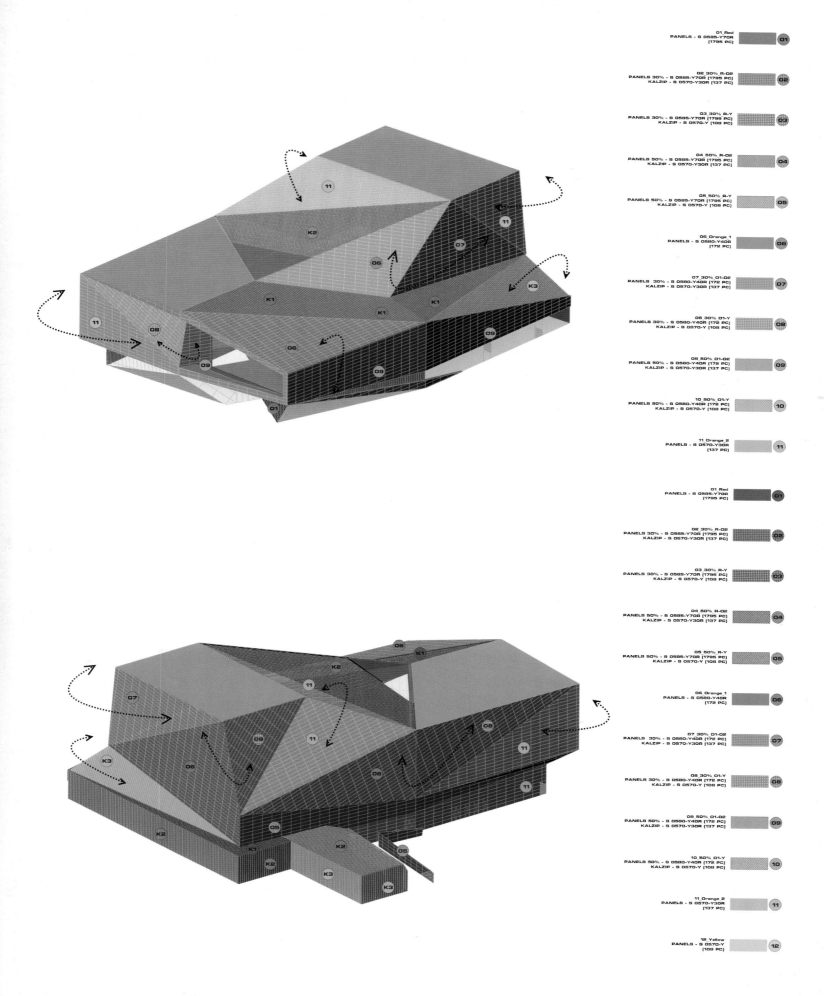

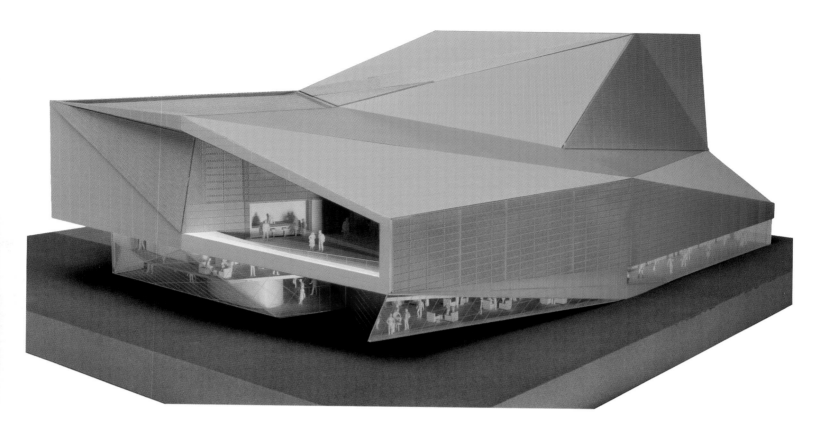

The wrapping surfaces of the theater give it a dynamic appearance that abandons the usual relationship between entrance façade, roof and walls.

Die Fassadenflächen verleihen dem Theater ein dynamisches Äußeres, das herkömmliche Kategorien wie Eingangsfassade, Dach und Wände überwindet.

Les surfaces enveloppantes du théâtre donnent une apparence dynamique qui remet en question les relations habituelles entre façade d'entrée, couverture et murs.

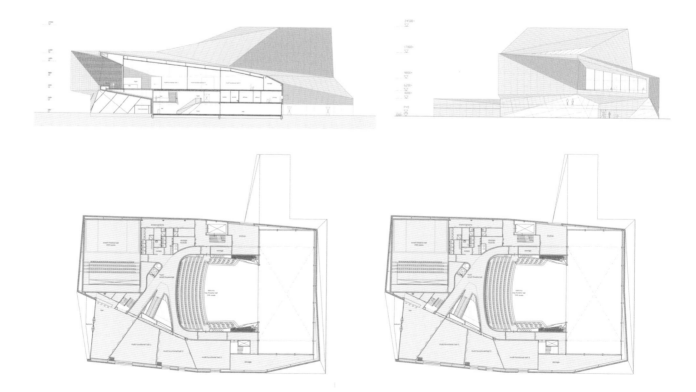

13

KOEN VAN VELSEN

KOEN VAN VELSEN
Spoorstraat 69a
1211 GA Hilversum

Tel: +31 35 6 22 20 00
Fax: +31 35 62 88 89 91
e-mail: kvv@architecten.A2000.nl

Born in Hilversum in 1952, **KOEN VAN VELSEN** graduated from the Academy of Architecture in Amsterdam in 1983. He started his own firm in Hilversum in 1977. His major works include the Discotheque Slinger, Hilversum (1978–79); the Van Velsen shop and house, Hilversum (1980–81); a public library, Zeewolde (1985–89); the Rijksakademie van Beeldende Kunsten, Amsterdam (1985–92); a multiplex cinema on Schouwburgplein, Rotterdam (1992–96); the Town Hall of Terneuzen (extension of the 1972 building by Van den Broek & Bakema, 1994–97); and the Film Academy, Amsterdam (1995–99). He has also worked on alterations of the Armamentarium, Delft (1982–89); the Ministry of Welfare, Public Health and Culture, Rijswijk (1985–86); and the Hotel Gooiland, Hilversum (1989–90). Van Velsen attempts to avoid a personal aesthetic, preferring to analyze each new project in its contextual, programmatic and other specific features, when proposing his designs.

MEDIA AUTHORITY BUILDING
HILVERSUM
1998 - 2002

FLOOR AREA: 2048 m²
CLIENT: Commissariaat voor de Media, Hilversum
COST: €3.42 million

Located 35 km south-east of Amsterdam, Hilversum is a wealthy town, where W. M. Dudok (1884–1974) built the town hall in the 1930s, and where Richard Meier erected his first building in the Netherlands, the KNP BT Headquarters (1987–92). Koen van Velsen is from Hilversum, where his Media Authority Building is located next to the Media Park. The structure was built with as much respect for the wooded site and for nature as possible. Patios have been cut into the building volume to avoid cutting down several existing trees. This is also true of the roof overhang, whose form was altered to make way for trees. Within the building, corridors are aligned along the two longer façades. Openings and large areas of glass on the façade offer glimpses of the surrounding landscape. Work areas, by contrast, face out onto internal patios that have been designed by the architect. Unlike the glass and metal exterior façades, the patio areas present "a differentiated composition of staggered windows, masonry walls and various splashes of color." Koen van Velsen acted in this instance as the architect, interior designer and landscape architect. His avowed intention is to create a feeling of calm and wellbeing, a goal that he apparently attained. With a floor area of 2048 m², the structure cost a total of €3.42 million.

Die wohlhabende Stadt Hilversum liegt 35 km südöstlich von Amsterdam. Willem Marinus Dudok (1884–1974) baute hier in den 1930er Jahren das Rathaus und Richard Meyer von 1987 bis 1992 sein erstes Gebäude in den Niederlanden, die KNP BT Hauptniederlassung. Koen van Velsen stammt aus Hilversum, und sein Media Authority Building liegt neben dem dortigen Media Park. Die Gestaltung respektiert weitgehend den Baumbestand und die natürliche Vegetation des Grundstücks. Innenhöfe wurden eingefügt, um das Abholzen von Bäumen zu vermeiden. Auch die Form des Dachüberstands wurde verändert, um Bäumen Platz zu machen. Im Inneren liegen Flure unmittelbar hinter den zwei längeren Fassa-den. Öffnungen und große Glasflächen bieten Ausblicke in die Landschaft. Im Gegensatz dazu sind die Arbeitsräume den Innenhöfen zugewandt, die ebenfalls vom Architekten gestaltet wurden. Anders als die Außenfassaden aus Glas und Metall präsentieren sich die Innenhöfe als eine „variationsreiche Komposition aus versetzt angeordneten Fenstern, Mauerwerkswänden und Flächen in unterschied-lichen Farben". Koen van Velsen war hier als Architekt, Innenarchitekt und Land-schaftsplaner tätig. Seine erklärte Absicht, ein Gefühl von Ruhe und Wohlbefinden zu erzeugen, hat er ganz offensichtlich verwirklichen können. Die Gesamtkosten für das Gebäude mit 2048 m² Geschossfläche betrugen 3,42 Millionen Euro.

À 35 km au sud-est d'Amsterdam, Hilversum est une ville aisée dont W. M. Dudok (1884–1974) avait édifié l'hôtel de ville dans les années 1930 et où Richard Meier a réalisé son premier projet aux Pays-Bas, le siège de KNP BT (1987–92). Koen van Velsen est originaire de cette ville où est situé l'immeuble de l'Autorité des médias près du Media Park. Le bâtiment a été construit dans le plus grand res-pect du terrain boisé et de la nature. Des patios ont été découpés dans le volume pour éviter d'avoir à abattre certains arbres. À l'intérieur, les corridors sont alignés dans l'axe des deux façades longues. Des ouvertures et de vastes surfaces vitrées permettent d'apercevoir le paysage environnant. Par contraste, les zones de travail donnent sur des patios intérieurs dessinés avec le plus grand soin. À la différence des façades extérieures en verre et métal, celles des patios présentent « une composition différenciée des fenêtres, des murs de maçonnerie et des différentes masses de couleurs étagées ». Koen van Vels a agit ici en tant qu'architecte, archi-tecte d'intérieur et paysagiste. Son intention revendiquée est de créer un sentiment de calme et de bien-être, objectif qu'il semble avoir atteint. D'une surface totale de 2048 m², ce bâtiment a coûté 3,42 millions d'euros.

An orchestration of windows, doors and volumes, which might bring to mind De Stijl, in some views, like the one above, actually participates in a very contemporary play on opacity and transparency, as seen in the entrance and façades to the left.

Die Komposition von Fenstern, Türen und Baumassen, die aus manchen Blickwinkeln (wie oben) an De Stijl erinnert, gehört zu einem sehr zeitgenössischen Spiel mit Transparenzgraden, wie man am Eingang und den Fassaden links im Bild sieht.

L'orchestration des fenêtres, des portes et des volumes – qui pourrait faire penser aux travaux du groupe De Stijl sous certains angles – participe à un jeu très contemporain sur l'opacité et la transparence, comme le montrent l'entrée et les façades à gauche.

KENNISPOORT
EINDHOVEN
2000 - 02

FLOOR AREA: 9700 m²
CLIENT: Technical University of Eindhoven
COST: €11.41 million

Built at the behest of the Technical University of Eindhoven (TU/e), with a gross floor area of 9700 m², Kennispoort is located in a park that separates the university from the city. The program includes offices, conference rooms, an information center, a restaurant and space for the local Chamber of Commerce. Both the location of the structure in the park and its elliptical shape were calculated to avoid future construction nearby at the expense of the greenery. Incisions in the building in the form of atria connect the floors. On the side of the Technical University, the elliptical plan has been altered to allow for a patio. Silver-glazed bricks cover a good part of the exteriors while iroko wood panelling has been used on floors, walls, stairs, columns and ceilings indoors. The cost of the structure was €11.41 million, excluding the interiors, also designed by Koen van Velsen. The southern Dutch city of Eindhoven (2004 pop. 208 000), heavily damaged during World War II, may be best known as the location of Philips, but it certainly has not developed the strong architectural tradition of Rotterdam, for example. Institutions such as the Witte Dame design center or the Van Abbe Museum do show that the city is fostering a culture of architecture, art and design, into which Koen van Velsen's building fits well.

Im Auftrag der Technischen Universität Eindhoven (TU/e) entstand Kennispoort mit 9700 m² Geschossfläche in einem zwischen Universität und Stadt gelegenen Park. Das Raumprogramm umfasst Büros, Konferenzräume, ein Informationszentrum, ein Restaurant und Räumlichkeiten für die Handelskammer. Sowohl die Lage des Gebäudes im Park als auch seine elliptische Form wurden so geplant, dass zukünftige Baumaßnahmen in der Nähe auf Kosten der Grünflächen vermieden werden. Einschnitte in das Gebäude in Form von Lichthöfen verbinden die Etagen. Zur Technischen Universität hin wurde der elliptische Grundriss verändert, um Platz für einen Innenhof zu schaffen. Silberfarben glasierte Ziegel bedecken einen Großteil der Außenfassade, im ebenfalls von Van Velsen entworfenen Innern finden sich Boden- und Treppenbeläge, Wand-, Stützen- und Deckenverkleidungen aus Iroko-Holz. Die südniederländische Stadt Eindhoven mit 208 000 Einwohnern (2004) wurde im Zweiten Weltkrieg schwer beschädigt und ist v. a. als Standort der Firma Philips bekannt, hat aber keine so bedeutende architektonische Tradition entwickelt wie etwa Rotterdam. Institutionen wie das Witte Dame Design Center oder das Van Abbe Museum zeugen jedoch davon, dass Eindhoven eine Kultur der Architektur, des Designs und der Kunst fördert, in die sich Koen van Velsens Gebäude gut einpasst.

Construit à la demande de l'Université technique d'Eindhoven (TU/e) et d'une surface totale de 9700 m², Kennispoort est implanté dans un parc qui sépare l'université de la ville. Le programme comprenait des bureaux, des salles de conférence, un centre d'information, un restaurant et des locaux pour la Chambre de commerce. L'implantation dans le parc comme la forme elliptique ont été calculées pour empêcher toute construction future aux dépens de l'espace vert. Les incisions dans le bâtiment en forme d'atriums connectent les différents niveaux. Du côté de l'Université, le plan elliptique a été modifié pour ouvrir un patio. La brique argentée habille une bonne part des façades extérieures tandis que des panneaux d'iroko recouvrent les sols, les murs, les escaliers, les colonnes et les plafonds. Le coût du projet s'est élevé à 11,41 millions d'euros, hors aménagements intérieurs, également conçus par Koen van Velsen. La ville d'Eindhoven (208 000 habitants en 2004), très endommagée pendant la Seconde Guerre mondiale et célèbre pour la présence de Philips, ne possède pas la forte tradition architecturale de Rotterdam, mais des institutions comme le centre de design Witte Dame ou le Van Abbe Museum montrent que la ville développe actuellement une culture d'architecture, d'art et de design dans lequel le projet de Koen van Velsen s'intègre parfaitement.

Geometric forms are cut out and repeated in varying patterns, giving a dynamic appearance to a building that might well otherwise have been quite dull.

Um den Bau dynamisch zu beleben, wurden an verschiedenen Stellen geometrische Formen aus dem Gebäudekörper ausge-schnitten.

Les formes géométriques découpées et répétées selon divers motifs donnent un aspect dynamique à un immeuble qui aurait pu paraître un peu ennuyeux.

Wood veneer columns and floor-to-ceiling glazing open this dining area (below) out toward the surrounding greenery. Slit windows are contrasted with large glazed bands, or unexpected voids.

Mit Furnierholz verkleidete Säulen und raumhohe Glaswände öffnen den Speisesaal (unten) zur grünen Umgebung. Fensterschlitze wechseln mit großen Bandfenstern oder – an unerwarteten Stellen – mit Lufträumen ab.

Des colonnes en bois verni et des baies toute hauteur ouvrent cette salle à manger (ci-dessous) sur la verdure environnante. D'étroites fenêtres contrastent avec de larges bandeaux vitrés ou des vides inattendus.

An unusual wood-clad space shows precisely how the architect carries over the themes expressed in the exterior of the building inside: cut outs and opaque surfaces give way to internal windows or other openings.

Ein ungewöhnlicher holzgetäfelter Raum verdeutlicht, wie der Architekt die Thematik der Außengestaltung im Gebäudeinneren fortführt: Einschnitte und opake Oberflächen setzen sich in Innenfenstern und anderen Wandöffnungen fort.

Un étonnant espace lambrissé de bois montre comment les architectes transposent les thèmes extérieurs à l'intérieur : les surfaces découpées ou opaques laissent place à des fenêtres internes ou à d'autres types d'ouvertures.

#14

RENÉ VAN ZUUK

RENÉ VAN ZUUK ARCHITEKTEN B. V.
De Fantasie 9
1324 HZ Almere

Tel: +31 36 5 37 91 39
Fax: +31 36 5 37 92 59
e-mail: info@renevanzuuk.nl
Web: www.renevanzuuk.nl

RENÉ VAN ZUUK received a Master of Sciences degree from the Technical University of Eindhoven (1988) and created his own firm in 1993. He has a design staff of five persons. Prior to that date, he worked for Skidmore, Owings & Merrill in London and Chicago (1988–89), Facilitair Bureau voor Bouwkunde in Rotterdam, and Hoogstad van Tilburg Architecten (1989–92). His notable completed projects include: ARCAM Architectural Center, Amsterdam (2003); Art Pavilion "De Verbeelding," Zeewolde (2001); Center for Plastic Arts "CBK," Alphen aan de Rijn (2000); Educational Farm "Griftsteede," Utrecht (1999); 4 Canal Houses, Java Island, Amsterdam (1997); Lock House "Oostersluis," Groningen (1995); Villa van Diepen, Almere (1995); and eight Bridges, Nieuwsloten (1993). Current work includes: Blok 16 housing and fitness complex, Almere (2003); Bridge for bicycles and pedestrians, Almere (2003); Bridge Keeper's House, Middelburg (unbuilt); and "Zilverparkkade" Office Building, Lelystad (2004).

ARCAM ARCHITECTUUR-CENTRUM AMSTERDAM 2002·03

FLOOR AREA: 477 m²
CLIENT: ARCAM
COST: €1.6 million

Located at the Oosterdok in Amsterdam, on Prins Hendrikkade not far from the Central Station, the Architectuurcentrum Amsterdam has a floor area of 477 m² and cost €1.6 million to build. ARCAM was set up as a foundation in 1986 and attempts to broaden the appeal of architecture, and to support and coordinate activities with other institutions. Built near the Metropolis Science Center by Renzo Piano, the three-level structure had to be as discreet as possible as seen from the nearby Shipping Museum. A zinc-finished aluminum Kalzip skin wraps around the building, together with a sloping glass façade. Inside, each part of the interior volume is connected to the others by voids, making all rooms "perceptible parts of the whole." The offices of the Arcam are on the top level, there is an exhibition space and information desk at the level of the Prins Hendrikkade and below, near the water, a level used for meetings and school groups. As the architect says, "Despite the limited measurements and the modest attitude of the building, the remarkable sculptural form will be responsible for the attention of this building in the historical site of the Oosterdok in the future."

Das Architekturzentrum Amsterdam befindet sich am Oosterdok in der Prins Hendrikkade unweit des Hauptbahnhofs und hat eine Gesamtfläche von 477 m². Die Baukosten beliefen sich auf 1,6 Millionen Euro. Das ARCAM wurde 1986 als Stiftung mit dem Ziel gegründet, ein breiteres Publikum für Architektur zu interessieren und mit anderen einschlägigen Institutionen zu kooperieren. Der dreigeschossige Bau in der Nähe von Renzo Pianos Metropolis Science Center sollte vom ebenfalls nahe gelegenen Schifffahrtsmuseum aus gesehen kaum auffallen. Er ist daher mit verzinktem Aluminiumblech (Marke Kalzip) verkleidet und hat geneigte verglaste Fassadenabschnitte. Jeder Innenraum ist durch Lufträume mit allen anderen Innenräumen verbunden, so dass alle separaten Bereiche deutlich wahrnehmbar Teile des Ganzen sind. Die Büros sind im obersten Stockwerk untergebracht, eine Ausstellungsgalerie und eine Informationstheke im Erdgeschoss und Konferenzräume sowie ein Seminarraum für Schülergruppen im Untergeschoss, das auf einer Höhe mit dem Wasserspiegel liegt. Der Architekt meint: „Trotz der geringen Ausmaße und Bescheidenheit des Gebäudes wird ihm seine auffallende skulpturale Form am historischen Oosterdok Aufmerksamkeit verschaffen."

Situé dans le quartier de l'Oosteerdok à Amsterdam, sur Prins Hendrikkade non loin de la gare centrale, le centre d'architecture d'Amsterdam offre une surface au sol de 477 m² pour un coût de construction de 1,6 million d'euros. ARCAM est une fondation créée en 1986 pour faire mieux connaître l'architecture en coordination avec d'autres institutions. Édifié non loin du centre des sciences Metropolis de Renzo Piano, le bâtiment de trois niveaux devait se fait aussi discret que possible. Une peau en zinc Kalsip à finition aluminium gaine le bâtiment dans lequel s'ouvrent deux façades inclinées en verre. À l'intérieur, chaque partie du volume se connecte aux autres par des vides ce qui fait de chaque salle « une partie perceptible de l'ensemble ». Les bureaux sont implantés au niveau supérieur tandis qu'à celui de la rue s'ouvrent une galerie d'exposition et un bureau d'information, et au bord de l'eau des espaces réservés aux réunions et à l'accueil de groupes scolaires. Pour René van Zuuk : « Malgré ses dimensions limitées et son aspect modeste, ce bâtiment en plein site historique de l'Oosterdok saura attirer l'attention par sa forme sculpturale originale. »

Within sight of Renzo Piano's New Metropolis
Science & Technology Center (1995-97),
the ARCAM building bends and twists until
its roof and walls are one and the same.
A modest structure, it shows what can be
done to enliven a small contemporary building.

In Sichtweite von Renzo Pianos Wissen-
schafts- und Technologiezentrum Metropolis
(1995–97) windet und schlängelt sich das
ARCAM-Gebäude so, dass Dach und
Fassaden eins werden. Der bescheidene Bau
demonstriert, wie man ein kleines
zeitgenössisches Gebäude ansprechend
gestalten kann.

Comment animer un bâtiment de dimensions modestes ? Non loin du Centre des
sciences et des technologies Metropolis de
Renzo Piano (1995–97), l'immeuble ARCAM
se courbe et se tord jusqu'à ce que ses murs
et sa toiture ne fassent plus qu'un.

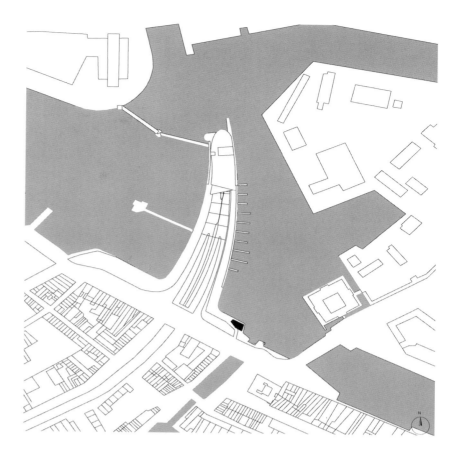

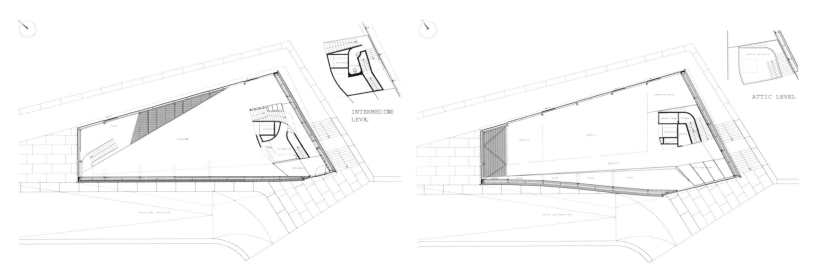

INTERMEDIATE LEVEL

ATTIC LEVEL

In spite of its rather quirky exterior, the ARCAM offers comfortable interior spaces, well adapted to the function of this architecture center.

Trotz seiner verschrobenen äußeren Form bietet das ARCAM im Inneren komfortable Räume, die perfekt auf die Funktion des Architekturzentrums zugeschnitten sind.

Malgré son extérieur un peu contourné, l'ARCAM offre des volumes intérieurs confortables bien adaptés à leur fonction de centre d'architecture.

BLOK 16
ALMERE
2002 - 04

FLOOR AREA: 8740 m²
CLIENT: Ontwikkelingscombinatie Almere Hart c. v.
COST: €5.6 million

Consisting of a block of 49 apartments and retail space, the Blok 16 complex, with a floor area of 8740 m², is part of the OMA master plan for the new center of Almere. The building's planning started in January 1999 and it was erected between December 2002 and October 2004 for a cost of €5.6 million. It is intended to mark the entrance to the harbor together with a structure designed by the architects Claus en Kaan. A curved deformation on the harbor side "flattens out towards the other end of the building, and adjusts to the orthogonal structure of the nearby housing towers by De Architecten Cie," confirming René van Zuuk's desire to make reference to neighboring architecture in his work, and also his interest in sculptural forms. This shape is also at the origin of the name of the building, "The Wave." Set on top of a parking garage, half of the ground floor is given over to commercial space and the rest to the entrance and storage areas for the apartments. The main staircase is set in a high open space, and all of the apartments in the building have living rooms on the southern side, facing the water. Aluminum-coated panels intended to change in appearance according to the direction of light enhance "the suggestion of movement initiated in the shape of the building," according to the architect.

Blok 16 hat eine Grundfläche von 8740 m², umfasst 49 Wohnungen sowie Ladenflächen und ist Teil des neuen Stadtzentrums von Almere, für das OMA den Masterplan erstellt hat. Im Januar 1999 begann Van Zuuk mit der Planung; der Bau erfolgte von Dezember 2002 bis Oktober 2004; die Baukosten beliefen sich auf 5,6 Millionen Euro. Zusammen mit einem Projekt von Claus en Kaan markiert Blok 16 das Tor zum Hafen. Eine geschwungene „Verformung" auf der Hafenseite „flacht sich zum anderen Ende des Gebäudes ab und passt sich der orthogonalen Struktur der benachbarten Wohnhochhäuser von De Architecten Cie. an". Dies bekräftigt René van Zuuks Bestreben, in seiner Arbeit stets Bezug auf Nachbarbauten zu nehmen, und entspricht seiner Vorliebe für plastische Formen. Die Bauform gab dem Gebäude auch seinen Namen „Die Welle". Das Erdgeschoss über der Tiefgarage wird zur Hälfte von Läden eingenommen, der Rest von der Eingangshalle und je einem Abstellraum pro Wohnung. Der Haupttreppenaufgang ist in einen hohen, offenen Raum eingestellt; alle Wohnungen haben Wohnzimmer mit Blick nach Süden, zum Wasser. Aluminiumbeschichtete Paneele, die je nach Lichteinfall changieren, unterstützen „die in der Form des Gebäudes angedeutete Bewegung", so der Architekt.

Ensemble de 49 appartements et de commerces, le Blok 16 (8740 m²) s'est intégré au plan directeur de OMA pour le nouveau centre de Almere. Sa conception a débuté en janvier 1999 et sa construction duré de décembre 2002 à octobre 2004 pour un budget de 5,6 millions d'euros. Avec une réalisation voisine du projet des architectes Claus en Kaan, cet immeuble marque l'entrée du port. La déformation en courbe observée du côté du port « s'aplatit vers l'autre extrémité de l'immeuble et s'ajuste aux structures orthogonales des tours de logements signées De Architecten Cie. », ce qui illustre le souhait de René van Zuuk de prendre en compte le contexte comme son intérêt pour les formes sculpturales. Cette forme justifie le nom de l'immeuble : « la Vague ». Au-dessus d'un parking, une moitié du rez-de-chaussée est consacrée à des commerces ainsi qu'à l'entrée de la partie résidentielle et le reste à des stockages pour les occupants. L'escalier principal occupe un espace ouvert de grande hauteur et chaque appartement possède un séjour donnant au sud, vers l'eau. Des panneaux aluminium enduit changent d'apparence en fonction de la lumière et créent, selon l'architecte, « la suggestion d'un mouvement initié par la forme du bâtiment ».

The scaled, leaning façade of the building together with its coloring give it an unusual, almost living appearance—as though it were in the process of moving in spite of its mass.

Die geschuppte geneigte Fassade und deren Farbgebung lassen das Gebäude fast wie ein Lebewesen aussehen, das sich trotz seiner Masse zu bewegen scheint.

La façade penchée de l'immeuble et sa coloration lui confèrent une apparence surprenante, presque vivante, comme s'il était prêt à se déplacer malgré sa masse.

The proximity of the building to the water's edge makes it seem as though the wind is making it move like a billowing sail.

Mit seiner Lage am Wasser wirkt das Gebäude wie ein vom Wind aufgeblähtes Schiffssegel.

La proximité de l'eau donne l'impression que l'immeuble est gonflé par le vent, comme une voile.

PHOTO CREDITS
IMPRINT

CREDITS PHOTOS / PLANS / DRAWINGS / CAD DOCUMENTS

18–23 top, 24–30 top, 31–33 top © janbitter.de / 23 bottom, 30 bottom, 33 bottom © Wiel Arets Architect / 34–38 top, 39 bottom, 41–44 top and center, 45–47 top, 48–49 © Christian Richters / 38 bottom, 39 top, 44 bottom, 47 bottom © Erick van Egeraat associated architects / 50–55, 58 bottom, 59 bottom, 60, 63 bottom © Architektuurstudio Herman Hertzberger / 57–58 top, 59 top, 61–63 top © Christian Richters / 64–70 top, 71 © Jeroen Musch / 70 bottom, 74 bottom © Meyer en van Schooten Architecten / 73–74 top, 75 © CIIID / Cees van Giessen / 76–91 © www.rob-thart.nl / 92–103 © Jeroen Musch / 104–113 © NOX/Lars Spuybroek / 114–127 © Christian Richters / 128–133 © ONL [Oosterhuis_Lénárd] / 134–156 top, 157, 158 bottom, 159–160 top, 161 © Christian Richters / 157 bottom, 158 top, 160 bottom, 147–165 © UN Studio / 166–177 © Duccio Malagamba / 178–182, 183 bottom, 184 top right and bottom, 185 bottom © Luuk Kramer fotografie / 184 top left © Markus Redert / 183 top, 185 top © René van Zuuk Architekten bv / 186–191 © Christian Richters

To stay informed about upcoming TASCHEN titles, please request our magazine at www.taschen.com/magazine or write to TASCHEN, Hohenzollernring 53, D-50672 Cologne, Germany, contact@taschen.com, Fax: +49-221-254919. We will be happy to send you a free copy of our magazine which is filled with information about all of our books.

© 2006 TASCHEN GmbH
Hohenzollernring 53, D–50672 Köln
www.taschen.com

PROJECT MANAGEMENT: Florian Kobler, Cologne
COLLABORATION: Barbara Huttrop, Cologne
PRODUCTION: Thomas Grell, Cologne
DESIGN: Sense/Net, Andy Disl and Birgit Reber, Cologne
GERMAN TRANSLATION: Annette Wiethüchter, Berlin
FRENCH TRANSLATION: Jacques Bosser, Paris

Printed in Italy
ISBN 3-8228-3971-X